An Exposition of...

The Gospel

of

JOHN

Revised Edition

Michael L. Gowens

Sovereign Grace Publications
Shallotte, North Carolina

AN EXPOSITION OF THE GOSPEL OF JOHN
(Revised Edition)
Published by Sovereign Grace Publications
Post Office Box 1150
Shallotte, North Carolina 28459
www.sovgrace.net
sovgracepublications@gmail.com

ISBN 978-1-929635-30-6

Scripture quotations are from the *King James Version* of the Bible.

Printed in the United States of America

Contents

Dedicated to Elder Bernard Gowens,
(my dad and father in the ministry)
a gentle, faithful servant of Christ
who recently celebrated the 50th Anniversary
of his ordination to gospel ministry (1968-2018).
Thank you for your consistent example of
sacrificial service to the people of God,
and for living before your family and
a watching world
a life of authentic Christian discipleship.

Introduction

Unlike the other three gospels, John's gospel is theological, not synoptic. Instead of giving a "play-by-play" narrative of the life and ministry of Jesus, John is more interested in explaining what the life of Christ means. He presents a classic Christology, a study of the person and work of the Lord Jesus Christ.

While Matthew & Luke begin with the birth of Jesus, and Mark with the personal ministry of Jesus, John begins with the preincarnate existence of Jesus as *"the Word who was in the beginning with God."* John's argument is that the works of Jesus identify Him as the eternal Son of God.

He is primarily concerned to present evidence for the deity of Jesus Christ. The key verse is 20:31: *"These are written that ye might believe that Jesus is the Christ, the Son of God..."* John wants to present Jesus in such a way as to bring people to gospel faith in Him as the one and only Son of God. This goal is sustained throughout the entire account.

Distinctive Features of John's Gospel

John aims to achieve this goal by recording seven miracles, five of which are not referenced in the other gospels; hence, some Bible students have referred to the Gospel of John as "the book of the seven signs." The seven miracles are: (1) Turning Water into Wine (2:1-11); (2) Healing the Nobleman's Son (4:46-54); (3) Curing the Impotent Man (5:1-9); (4) Feeding the Five Thousand (6:5-14); (5) Walking on Water (6:16-21); (6) Restoring Sight to the Man Born Blind (9:1-7); and (7) Resurrecting Lazarus (11:1-45). These miracles prove that Jesus was more than a man – indeed, that He was God manifest in the flesh. Each demonstrates some aspect of His sovereignty – over disability (#1), distance (#2), disease (#3), difficulties (#4), domicile (#5), darkness (#6), and death (#7).

In addition to the seven signs, John records eleven "I Am" statements of Jesus. He claims, "I am…the bread of life (6:35), the light of the world (8:12), the door of the sheepfold (10:9), the good shepherd (10:11), the resurrection and the life (11:25), the way, truth and life (14:6), and the true vine (15:1)."

The passage in John 8:51-58 explains that Jesus, by employing the title "I Am", was claiming identity with the eternally present and preexistent God of Abraham. The Jews got the message, for they immediately "took up stones to cast at him" for blasphemy.

John's gospel record contains several discourses of our Lord that do not appear in the other gospels. The chief of these sermons is the last sermon he ever delivered—a discourse to his disciples on the heels of the Last Supper, recorded in John 14-16.

It also records the high-priestly, intercessory prayer our Lord offered on behalf of his disciples in the shadow of the cross (Jno. 17). It is the sole account of this prayer in the New Testament.

Responding to John's Gospel

John's gospel account demonstrates that some, compelled by the evidence, will come to gospel faith in the Lord Jesus Christ, and some will not. Some "received him" (1:12; 3:33; 4:45; 17:8) and "believed on him" (1:7; 1:12; 4:42; 6:29-30; 6:69; 7:39; 9:35-38; 10:37-38; 11:15; 11:27; 11:40, 42; 11:48; 12:36; 13:19; 14:1; 14:11; 14:29; 16:30-31; 17:20-21; 19:35; 20:31). Others "received him not" (1:11; 3:11; 5:43) and "believed not" (3:12; 4:48; 5:38; 5:44-47; 6:36; 6:64; 7:5; 8:24; 8:45-46; 9:18; 10:26; 12:39; 12:47; 16:9; 20:25).

John presents evangelical belief in the Lord Jesus Christ as both an evidence that a person possesses eternal life (3:15-18; 3:36; 5:24; 6:47; 11:25-26) and the means by which a person might partake of the joys of an abundant life even now (6:35; 6:40; 7:38; 12:46; 14:12; 20:31). As we study this thrilling gospel account, may we respond in a true confession of faith like Thomas, saying, *"My Lord and my God."*

Introduction

Chapter 1
Prologue (John 1:1-18)

The prologue to John's Gospel, recorded in the first eighteen verses of chapter 1, is a theological summary of the book's theme. In a logical progression of argument, John builds an irrefutable case for the deity of Jesus Christ.

Notice how he begins by speaking of "the Word" (1:1), and logically proceeds to "personalize" the Word (1:14a), then to identify this Word as "the only begotten Son" (1:14b), and finally to identify Him by name as "Jesus Christ" (1:17). Interestingly, after identifying the Word as the Son in verse 14, John does not refer to Him as "the Word" again, but only as "the Son."

Why does John cease to call Him "the Word" after verse 14? Did the Son cease to be the Word? No. The title, however, has served its purpose. John employs the title in order to capture the minds of both his Jewish and his Greek readers. Both Jews and Gentiles would have agreed, at least at an abstract, philosophical level, that there existed a principle of "logic" or rationality in the universe. The word employed for "Word" is *logos*, from which the English concept of "logic" is derived.

When John's Jewish readers heard his opening sentence – "In the beginning was the Word" – they would have recalled Psalm 33:6: *"By the word of the Lord were the heavens made and all the host of them by the breath of his mouth,"* and Proverbs 8 where the abstract concept of "wisdom" is credited with the act of creation.

When his Gentile (or Greek) readers heard that sentence, they would have thought of the principle of wisdom, reason, logic, and order that permeates the created world. All of their great philosophers—Plato, Socrates, Aristotle and the rest— taught that a great Mind of Reason stood in back of the universe and that the structure and order and rationality observable in the world testified to that fact. The disciplines of mathematics and science derive from this concept of the *Logos*.

So, by beginning his gospel with the abstract principle of the *Logos*, John engaged the ear of both his Jewish and his Greek readers. When he says, then, "In the beginning was the Word, and the Word was with God, and the Word was God" (1:1), both his Jewish and his Gentile auditors would have responded, "Amen". They would also agree with the abstract premise that this Word was the Creator (1:3) and the source of knowledge and enlightenment (1:4 – theologians refer to this as "natural revelation" or "the moral law"—cf. Ps. 19:1ff).

Verses six through eight (1:6-8), however, mark a dramatic turning point in the case that John is building. In these verses, he moves from the theoretical to the historical – from the abstract to the concrete: *"There was a man sent from God, whose name was John."*

Again, both Jewish and Gentile readers would affirm John's historical point of reference. "Yes," the Greeks would say, for they could not dispute the historical existence of this man named John the Baptist. The Jews also would agree, for they took John to be a true prophet of God.

Verses nine through thirteen (1:9-13) take the argument even a step further as John develops the thought that John the Baptist testified of and pointed to "the true Light". By verse fourteen (1:14), the apostle has set up his readers for an inescapable conclusion. The Word is a Person!

"The Word was made flesh and dwelt among us..." In this verse, John personalizes this abstract concept and states that this "flesh and blood human being" is at one and the same time "the only begotten" Son of God: *"...and we beheld his glory, the glory as of the only begotten of the Father, full of grace and truth."*

Twice in the passage (vs. 14 & 18), John refers to Him as "the only begotten". This combination of adjectives speaks of Him as "the unique One, the one and only, the one of a kind". In contrast to those who are "sons of God" by the new birth (1:13) and those who manifest their sonship by believing (1:12), Jesus is the unique Son of God. He is not God's Son by natural birth, new birth, or special creation, but by virtue of His essential oneness with the Father (cf. v. 18 – "in the bosom of the Father").

Then, in verse seventeen (1:17), John identifies this Incarnate Word who is God's unique Son, and to whom John the Baptist pointed, by the name "Jesus Christ". Verse fifteen (1:15) teaches that the Son, though existing before, yet came after John the Baptist. Verse sixteen (1:16) identifies the Son as the source of all blessings. Verse seventeen (1:17) names Him "Jesus Christ." Verse eighteen (1:18) identifies Him as co-equal, co-essential, and co-eternal with the Father.

If you've stayed with me in this logical progression of thought, you are likely spellbound by the profundity of John's argument. By identifying the Son of God as "Jesus Christ", John implies that everything he has been saying about "the Word" (i.e. the Word is eternal God, the Creator and source of all knowledge) is true about Jesus, and everything he has said about the Son (i.e. the Son is the Word incarnate, the One and only of the Father, the Source of all blessings and the Revealer of the Father) is also true about Jesus.

In a word, John builds a case for the point that Jesus is God. He is the Creator, the Light, and Revealer of God. The prologue to John's Gospel is a powerful and incontrovertible exegesis of the deity of Jesus Christ.

Chapter 2
John the Baptist (John 1:19-34)

The case John builds for the Deity of Jesus Christ begins with this passage concerning the ministry of John the Baptist. Verses 19-34 embellish the introduction already given in the prologue (1:6). Unlike the synoptic Gospels, however, John goes into no detail concerning how he was dressed, what he ate, or how he preached a message of repentance. His sole concern is to establish that John the Baptist recognized and witnessed to the deity of Jesus.

Messiah's Forerunner

Most people tend to overlook the importance of John the Baptist. He is overshadowed—and rightly so—by the One to whom he witnessed, the Lord Jesus Christ. But had he lived in Old Testament times, outside the shadow of the One to whom he deferred, John the Baptist would have been heralded as another Isaiah, Jeremiah or Daniel.

Yet John the Baptist had no personal ambitions or aspirations. He was content to fulfill one mission and one mission only. His sole reason for existing was to "prepare the way of the Lord" (Is. 40:3; Mr. 1:2-3), to announce the coming King.

In ancient times, a "forerunner" was sent in advance to announce a monarch's arrival (2 Sam. 15:1). It was his job to notify the people that a dignitary was near, to encourage them to make the necessary preparations and to "roll out the red carpet", so to speak. John was commissioned by God to perform this task for the Messianic King. He would "make ready a people prepared for the Lord" (Lk. 1:17) by calling them to repentance at the grass-roots level of their family relationships (Mal. 4:5-6). Only then would they be ready to hear the more "spiritual" message of Jesus.

The language of Isaiah 40:4-8 indicates that he would address everyone on the same level – as frail and feeble sinners. Neither the high hills of aristocratic privilege nor the deep valleys of lowly misery would alter his message. All would be addressed as equally deficient – "All flesh is grass and the goodliness thereof, as the flower of the field." None would be exempt from the relevance of John's message.

According to Luke 16:16, John the Baptist was a pivotal figure in redemptive history. He was the last of the Old Testament prophets, but also the herald of the New dispensation. When Jesus editorializes of John's greatness of character in Matthew 11, he emphasizes that great character is only eclipsed by great privilege – "...nevertheless he that is least in the kingdom of heaven is greater than he" (v. 11).

Perhaps the greatest characteristic of John the Baptist was his humility. To experience the kind of success he enjoyed without allowing such success to cloud his perspective is truly an impressive feat.

John was a charismatic leader who gathered around himself an impressive entourage of loyal disciples. So significant was the movement he led that the religious leaders sent a delegation to ask him who he was (1:19). John resisted any temptation, however, to exaggerate his own importance. "And he confessed, and denied not; but confessed, I am not the Christ" (1:20).

When they further pressed him whether or not he was Elijah or "that prophet" (probably a reference to the prophecy in Deut. 18:18), he stated point-blank, "I am not" (1:21). Instead he identifies himself simply as "the voice of one crying in the wilderness" (1:23).

A "voice" is something one hears, but does not see. John was willing to remain inconspicuous because he knew that the work he had been commissioned to do was not about him. Such a self-effacing mindset is crucial to every gospel minister. Our principle task is to point others to the Lord Jesus Christ, not to draw attention to ourselves. Taking his cue years later from the Baptist's example, Paul would say, "For we preach not ourselves, but Christ Jesus the Lord" (2 Cor. 4:5; cf. 1 Cor. 2:1-3).

When the Pharisees pressed him why he was baptizing followers if he had no intention of forming a movement around himself as its center (1:25), John witnessed to the superiority and preeminence of Christ: "There standeth one among you, whom ye know not [an illusion to vs. 10-11 in the prologue]; He it is, who coming after me is preferred before me, whose shoe's latchet I am not worthy to unloose." It is as if John can find no expression powerful or descriptive enough to explain the distance between him and the One to whom he pointed. So he chooses this image of a servant removing his master's sandals. John confesses his unworthiness to even perform this most menial of tasks.

John the Baptist understood the nature of the task before him – to witness to the Lord Jesus Christ. He fulfilled that task willingly, without succumbing to the temptation to believe his own press-clippings or to claim any special favors for himself. As such, he stands as a sterling example of faithfulness in ministry to everyone who would follow in his steps. There is no greater employ than the call to witness to the Lord Jesus. There is no higher privilege than to be a simple "voice", crying in the wilderness of this world that the glory of man is like a fading flower, but that the Word of God, the eternal *Logos*, will stand forever.

John the Baptist's Message

The day following John's testimony to the Jewish delegation, Jesus approached John to be baptized. Our Lord was baptized by John the Baptist not because he was a sinner who needed cleansing but to "fulfill all righteousness" (cf. Mt.

3:15) and to blaze the trail as the "author of our faith" for entrance into the kingdom of God. Every true follower of the Lord Jesus Christ should follow in the Savior's steps by submitting to gospel baptism. This moment marked the inception of the gospel church.

As Jesus approached, John proclaimed the first gospel sermon of the gospel dispensation: *"Behold the Lamb of God which taketh away the sin of the world"* (v. 29). We may learn several important lessons about what it means to be a Gospel witness from these words.

First, it is important that the gospel witness be verbal. Though we often speak of the importance of witnessing by our walk and example, such non-verbal testimony does not substitute for the necessity of a verbal witness. It still pleases God by the foolishness of preaching—not programs, plays, projects, or productions—to save them that believe (1 Cor. 1:21). The verbal proclamation of the gospel is still the chief business of and most potent weapon in the church's arsenal.

Secondly, a true and effective gospel witness must proclaim a true and accurate message. It's not enough to simply say something about Christ. The truth of who he is and what he came to do is essential.

John identifies him as "the Lamb of God". This title emphasizes his sacrificial and redemptive purpose and pinpoints Jesus as the fulfillment of Old Testament prophecy. The Jews looked for someone to lead a revolution against

Rome, but Jesus came not to establish a political kingdom, but to die as a sacrifice for sin.

All the sacrifices of the Old Testament anticipated this moment. Abel's sacrifice of a firstling of his flock (Gen. 4) foreshadowed him, as did Abraham's reassurance to Isaac that God would provide himself a lamb for a burnt offering (Gen. 22:9), the Israelite's offering of a firstborn lamb without blemish at the first Passover (Ex. 12), and Isaiah's prophecy that Messiah would be led as a lamb to the slaughter (Is. 53:7). Every lamb offered as a burnt offering or trespass offering throughout the 1500 years of Levitical worship typified this One whom John identifies as God's Lamb.

Why is Jesus called "God's Lamb"? Because he is God's provision for sinners—the ultimate sin offering for people who need to be rescued from the consequences of sin. That God would provide the sacrifice necessary to save men from their own sins is a testimony to His amazing grace.

There are other thoughts involved in this blessed title. First, there is a hint of his sinlessness, for God required that the lamb devoted to sacrificial service be holy and without blemish (cf. 1 Pet. 1:19). It also suggests the voluntary nature of his sacrifice. A lamb is dumb as he is led to the slaughter. Likewise, the Lord Jesus never opened his mouth in his own defense. He laid down his life—no man took it from him (cf. Jno. 10:18). He died willingly and voluntarily, not by coercion or constraint. Further, it suggests the substitutionary nature of his sacrifice. The lamb in Levitical worship died in the place of the worshippers. Likewise, the Redeemer would die a vicarious death, in the room and stead of those he represented.

What would the Lamb of God accomplish? He would "take away" sin. He would not merely delay the consequences of it, or temporarily conceal it. He would "put it away by the sacrifice of himself" (cf. Heb. 9:26). He would "separate it from us as far as the east is from the west" (Ps. 103:12), "blot it out as a thick cloud" (Is. 44:22), "cast it into the depths of the sea" (Micah 7:19), "sealed it up and sewn it in a bag" (Job 14:17), and "cast it behind his back" (Is. 38:17).

For whom would he do this? He would take away the sin "of the world" — that is, for Gentiles as well as Jews. This is the first reference to the concept of "the world" in John's Gospel, an expression that must be defined in terms of its context. Seldom does a reference to "the world" in Scripture mean "all without exception". Most of the time it means "all without distinction". In other words, seldom does "the world" speak of every man, woman, boy and girl who has lived, lives now, or will live in the future. Instead, it means all classes or kinds, without distinction of race, class, color or creed. In this passage, as elsewhere in John's Gospel, it describes a benefit that would extend not only to Jews but also to Gentiles. Under the Law, only Jews were privileged and advantaged (cf. Rom. 3:1). But in Christ, those religious distinctions are removed. Gentiles as well as Jews who are

15

elect of God would be represented in his sacrificial death on Calvary.

Those who insist that expressions like this be interpreted in terms of a universal or a general atonement face a very difficult problem. The text actually says too much for them. It indicates that the Lamb would actually "take away" their sins. He would not merely make it possible for sin to be removed if they will contribute some further act, such as repentance, baptism or faith, to his sacrifice. He would actually "take sin away". So, if this expression refers to all men without exception, then it follows that all men without exception have the benefit of having their sins taken away. On what basis, then, would anyone be condemned to eternal punishment? If one for whom Christ died perishes, he will perish without his sins, for they have been taken away.

Some suggest that Jesus put away the sins of all men but if they refuse to accept it and believe it then they will be lost forever. But I would ask, "Is not unbelief a sin as well as lust, pride, drunkenness and murder?" Did Jesus simply take away every sin except the sin of unbelief, or did he also successfully remove that sin as well? Obviously, even the sin of unbelief was "taken away" by God's Lamb, when he died for his people on the cross.

The Baptism of Jesus (1:31-34)

This passage makes mention of three "baptisms": the baptism of John, the baptism of Jesus (a template and precursor for Christian baptism), and the baptism of the Holy Spirit.

John's Baptism

John reveals the purpose of his baptism in verse 31: *"And I knew him not: but that he should be made manifest to Israel, therefore am I come baptizing with water."* John came baptizing his subjects with "the baptism of repentance" (Mt. 3:11) to prepare the "repenters" to receive the ministry of the Lord Jesus Christ. The ultimate objective of John's baptism, then, was (1) to identify the truly penitent, (2) to identify the Messiah, and (3) to match-make these penitents with the Lord Jesus Christ.

Neither his ministry nor his baptism, therefore, were ever intended to be permanent. John's baptism was a transitional form of baptism between the ceremonially "washings" of the old law and gospel or believers baptism. Once the Messiah was identified, John's primary purpose was fulfilled and satisfied. The momentum he built prior to this moment would gradually fade as more and more of his followers transferred allegiance to the Lord Jesus Christ. John knew that he must decrease while Christ increased (cf. 3:30).

The reference to the baptism of Jesus is in verse 32: *"And John bare record, saying, I saw the Spirit descending from heaven like a dove, and it abode upon him"*. The occasion to which John

17

refers is the baptism of Jesus. John cites this episode as evidence for the deity of Christ. That the Holy Spirit would descend like a dove and abide on Jesus displays Heaven's endorsement and identification of Jesus as the anticipated Messiah and Son of God.

Matthew tells us that this heavenly endorsement was followed by an audible voice from heaven saying, *"This is my beloved Son in whom I am well pleased"* (Mt. 3:17). God the Father turned the spotlight fully and completely on Jesus. Those who had responded to John's ministry would now have their focus redirected to the One for whose sake John's labor was merely preparatory.

The baptism of Jesus is the prototype of gospel, or Christian, baptism. Just as an assurance of sonship was given ("This is my beloved Son"), so gospel baptism provides "the answer of a good conscience toward God" (1 Pet. 3:21). And just as God was "well pleased", so the subject of gospel baptism can know that this act of obedience is pleasing to the Lord.

In gospel baptism, a penitent believer identifies himself with the Lord Jesus Christ. He says by this act that he wants to follow in the steps of Jesus. Further he confesses his confidence in and dependence on the death, burial and resurrection of Christ as the sole ground and basis of his salvation, for baptism depicts death, burial and resurrection.

The Baptism of the Holy Spirit

In verse 33, John makes reference to the baptism of the Holy Ghost: *"...He that sent me to baptize with water, the same said unto me, Upon whom thou shalt see the Spirit descending, and remaining on him, the same is he which baptizeth with the Holy Ghost"*.

It is interesting that no mention is here made of Christ "baptizing with fire", as Matthew 3:11 indicates. Such is obviously a reference to the final judgment on the wicked at the last day. Christ will be the administrator of that "final" baptism. But he is also the administrator of the baptism with the Holy Spirit prior to that time.

What is this "baptism with the Holy Ghost"? It is possible that this is a theological reference to the work of regeneration, as 1 Corinthians 12:13 indicates. Because the work of quickening sinners into new life had been going on since there was an elect on this earth, however, I favor the interpretation that this is an historical reference to the outpouring of the Holy Ghost in his new covenant ministry – "the gift of the Holy Ghost" if you please (Acts 2:38). That ministry began at Pentecost (Acts 2) and will continue until the Lord Jesus returns in glory.

Chapter 3
Before Philip Called Thee (John 1:35-51)

This passage records the first gospel converts to the Lord Jesus Christ. They were Andrew, Simon Peter, Philip and Nathanael. Andrew and Peter were brothers, while Philip and Nathanael were friends.

Some Bible readers have recognized what appears to be a contradiction between this passage and Mark 1:16-20. Here, Jesus first meets with Andrew who in turn summons his brother Peter and brings him to Jesus. In Mark's account, however, Jesus encounters both brothers "casting a net into the sea" and exhorts, *"Come ye after me and I will make you to become fishers of men."* Is this a contradiction in the gospel record?

The answer is "no." It is clear that the passage in Mark records their "call to ministry" and the passage before us in John records their gospel conversion. Obviously their conversion occurred first and the call to service was subsequent to that.

Conversion & Regeneration

Conversion is a theological term referring to a change of mind. We properly distinguish it from regeneration, which is a change of nature. Regeneration must necessarily precede conversion, as life must precede action. So, conversion to the gospel is something subsequent to regeneration, and is an evidence that the new birth has already occurred. Consider the earlier passage in John 1:12-13 where verse twelve speaks of people who *"received Him"* and *"believed on His name"* — language that describes what happens in gospel conversion — and verse thirteen indicates that such converts have *already* been born again.[1] It is important to note that the work of regeneration (or the effectual call) has eternal consequence, while gospel conversion (or the gospel call) relates to serving the Lord in a life of discipleship in this life.

Andrew and Peter

The first disciples of Jesus were originally disciples of John the Baptist. As Jesus passed by, John the Baptist again exclaimed, *"Behold the Lamb of God"* (1:36). At that, the two disciples, one of whom was Andrew, followed Jesus. When Jesus questioned their intentions, they asked, *"Master, where dwellest thou?"* Jesus responded, *"Come and see."*

Obviously, they wanted to know where Jesus lived, i.e. his place of physical residence. And Jesus took them to his

---

[1] Also see Jno. 5:24, 1 Jno. 5:1, 1 Pet. 1:21a, etc. (as well as the example of Cornelius in Acts 10) indicating that regeneration precedes gospel faith.

physical dwelling where they stayed with him the remainder of the day. Before the passage is finished, however, it is clear that the answer to this question, i.e. Where are you from?, is more in depth than it might first appear. John 1:51 indicates that the real home of this intriguing Man was heaven and that the real identity of this Man could not be determined simply by visiting his physical place of abode.

Andrew and this unnamed man (most suppose the second person is John, the writer of this gospel account) arrived at the residence of Jesus at "about the tenth hour," or near 4:00 p.m. They stayed with him the rest of the day. No record is given of their conversation, but it is safe to assume that their eyes were opened and their hearts burned within them, for the next day, Andrew went immediately to his brother Simon Peter and told him, *"We have found the Messiah"* (1:41).

Conversion involves "finding (or discovering) Christ", while regeneration is a matter of Christ finding the individual (Deut. 32:10; see Eze. 16). In conversion, men are the "seekers" (1:38), but in regeneration, the Lord is the One doing the seeking (Lk. 19:10). In conversion people are "brought to Jesus" (1:42a) or they "come to Jesus" (1:47), but in regeneration, Jesus comes to them. It is interesting to note in the Gospels that though the sick, diseased, and troubled often came or were brought to Jesus for healing, the dead never were. Jesus always went to the dead. So it is in regeneration.

When Peter came to the Lord, Jesus immediately changed his name from Simon, meaning "shifting sand", to Cephas (or

Peter), meaning "a stone." Obviously Jesus gave him a name that suggested the thought of stability of character with a view of helping this new convert to grow into the name. Anyone who knows the story of Peter's process of spiritual maturation can understand how the Lord did indeed develop spiritual stability in this initially unsteady and impetuous individual.

There is an instructive practical lesson here concerning the importance of witnessing to one's own family members. Peter was Andrew's brother. I suspect Christian people often miss the best opportunities to influence others with the gospel because they overlook the people who are closest to them. The best gospel labor does not take place in a large public gathering but in the family living room. Home is still the best place in the world to impact others for the glory of the God.

Philip and Nathanael

The next day, Jesus summoned Philip, an acquaintance of Peter and Andrew, to follow him. Philip in turn found his close friend Nathanael and said, *"We have found him, of whom Moses in the law, and the prophets, did write, Jesus of Nazareth, the son of Joseph"* (1:45). But Nathanael is skeptical. His prejudice is an obstacle to faith: *"Can any good thing come out of Nazareth?"* he asks. Instead of scolding him for prejudice, or entering into some elaborate debate to prove that Nazareth had a few redeeming qualities, Philip simply responds, *"Come and see"* (1:46).

This simple invitation is frequently more effective than rhetoric and argument. See for yourself, he exhorts—an invitation that was at once designed to both overcome his skepticism and peak his interest. The principle here is that some things are better felt than told—that personal experience is sometimes more compelling than logical argument.

As Nathanael came to Christ, Jesus announces that He had already come to Nathanael: *"Behold an Israelite indeed, in whom is not guile!"* (1:47). That Jesus knew him was a surprise to Nathanael. *"Whence knowest thou me?"* Nathanael asks. In modern vernacular, he wants to know, "Have we met?" Jesus' response is telling: *"Before that Philip called thee, when thou wast under the fig tree, I saw thee."* (1:48)

What happened to Nathanael "under the fig tree"? We are not told. Evidently, it was an experience that Nathanael remembered. Perhaps it was a deeply personal moment—a private experience in which he had experienced something profoundly moving and salutary. Maybe he was under deep conviction for his sin and cried out in the depths of his soul for mercy. Whatever Nathanael felt under the fig tree, it is evident that Jesus knew all about it and that it was here that Jesus had met Nathanael.

Notice that this experience with the Lord took place "before Philip called" him. The Lord arrived on the scene before the evangelist! Regeneration preceded gospel conversion! So it is in the case of every one who has ever had his eyes opened to see the Lamb of God. Before you saw Him, He saw you.

This revelation was enough for Nathanael. He answered in the language of gospel confession, *"Rabbi, thou art the Son of God; thou art the King of Israel."* (1:49)

Seeing Jacob's Ladder (1:50-51)

"Jesus answered and said unto him, Because I said unto thee, I saw thee under the fig tree, believest thou? Thou shalt see greater things than these. And he saith unto him, Verily, verily, I say unto you, Hereafter ye shall see heaven open, and the angels of God ascending and descending upon the Son of man." John 1:50-51

The verses that conclude John 1 are obviously a promise – but what, specifically, do they promise? To what, exactly, do these verses refer?

First, they contain *the promise of increasing delight in true Christian experience.* Nathanael marveled at the display of Christ's omniscience but Jesus indicated that there were more marvelous revelations to come. Because our Lord is incomprehensible, we can never sound the depths or explore the farthest reaches of His infinite glory. True Christian experience is one ongoing enjoyment, at ever-deepening levels, of delight in Christ. About the point that we think the subject is exhausted, the Lord reveals that there is more to come.

Second, these verses refer to *the mediatorial work of the Lord Jesus Christ.* The imagery employed, i.e. angels ascending and

26

descending, is reminiscent of Jacob's ladder. In Genesis 28, Jacob dreamed of a ladder, the bottom of which touched the earth and the top, the heaven. On this ladder connecting heaven and earth, angels descended (obviously dispatched from God's throne to carry out some mission on the earth – cf. Heb. 1:14) and ascended (obviously, returning back to heaven for a new assignment once the previous one was complete).

The picture Jacob saw, then, is a picture of Divine Providence. There is activity on this ladder. God is not remote and disconnected from Jacob's life, as he might have previously thought, but active and involved. The angels are agents of Divine providence, sent to carry out certain orders, perpetually involved in the lives of those who are the heirs of grace. Providence is the connecting link between heaven and earth.

By taking this familiar language and applying it to Himself – *"...hereafter ye shall see the angels of God ascending and descending upon the Son of man"* – the Lord Jesus claims to be the ultimate expression of God's providential involvement in the lives of human beings. Christ is the antitype of Jacob's ladder – the connecting link between heaven and earth – the One Mediator between God and men (1 Tim. 2:5). He is God's provision for sinners and the One through whom "all spiritual blessings" flow toward His people (Eph. 1:3; Rom. 8:32).

Jesus tells Nathanael that in time he would witness the fulfillment of the vision God gave to Jacob thousands of years previous. Obviously this is a promise of the cross and the mediatorial work of salvation Christ would accomplish on behalf of all who were given to Him by the Father before time began. In Nathanael's mind at that point, Jesus was an omniscient teacher, the Divine Son of God, Israel's King (cf. v. 49). He would eventually come to view Him, however, as the Savior of sinners and the means of every spiritual blessing to His children (v. 51). That is indeed a "greater thing" to see.

Finally, the promise here probably also refers to *the future and glorious return of the Lord Jesus Christ*. Quite literally, the heavens will be opened and angels will accompany the Lord at His return (Rev. 19:11-16). The second coming of the Lord Jesus Christ will be, without a doubt, the greatest spectacle ever observed. Not only will Nathanael see it, but "every eye shall see Him, even those that pierced Him" (Rev. 1:7). It will be a day of great rejoicing for God's children, and a day of terrible doom for the wicked.

Nathanael's conversion experience had been a special blessing in his life. Our Lord acknowledges that fact, but then adds that there was more to come. To those who have seen the omniscient Christ as the one Mediator between God and men and the only means (or instrument) through which all spiritual benefits flow into their lives, the prospect that the greatest spectacle of all is yet future, i.e. the Redeemer's glorious return, is sufficient to keep them moving forward in faith to that happy and triumphant day.

Chapter 4

The Beginning of Miracles (John 2:1-17)

John 2:1-11 records the first of seven miracles in John's Gospel – the miracle of turning water to wine at the marriage feast in Cana of Galilee. Cana was the hometown of Nathanael and the invitation of Jesus and his disciples to this festive occasion probably came through him.

The Occasion of the Miracle

On first glance, it appears that this miracle is different than Jesus' other miracles. No sickness is remedied; no real crisis, as we would ordinarily consider a crisis, is averted; no individual is really helped. Unlike Jesus' other miracles, no demon is cast out; no leper is cleansed; no storm at sea is calmed.

In fact, the occasion of this miracle might be considered, at least on the surface, to be somewhat mundane and beneath the spiritual dignity of Jesus' ministry. Jesus attends a festive occasion and solves a minor inconvenience on behalf of the host and for the enjoyment of the wedding guests. On closer examination, however, this miracle teaches several practical lessons that are perfectly consistent with the character of Jesus' ministry.

Practical Lessons

First, the setting of this miracle teaches *the value that our Lord places on the covenant of marriage*. Marriage was ordained of God in creation as one of the building blocks of an orderly society. As a creation ordinance, it is a moral, not necessarily a religious, institution. In other words, marriage is not an ordinance of the church but of society; hence, civil law recognizes wedding ceremonies performed by judges, ship captains, and military officers as equally valid to those performed by ordained ministers of the gospel.

The New Testament, however, indicates that the best marriage is a Christian marriage, one that reflects the relationship that exists between Christ and the Church (see Eph. 5). When two believers marry "in the Lord" (1 Cor. 7:39), they have added resources and incentive for the kind of sacrificial love, life-long fidelity and commitment that is so crucial to marital success. I find it extremely significant that one of our Lord's first acts of public ministry was to attend a wedding festival bringing blessing to that occasion by his presence.

Secondly, we learn here that *spirituality does not mean isolation from the secular world*. Serving the Lord does not involve separating oneself from every activity that is not specifically religious. Over and again, we are warned that serving Christ does not mean that a person must live as a monk, sequestered in a cloistered community away from ordinary affairs (cf. 1 Cor. 5:10). Jesus prayed not that God would take his disciples "out of the world" but "keep them from the evil" (Jno. 17:15). It is no sin to enjoy life, for God "has given us richly all things to enjoy" (1 Tim. 6:17). In fact, the Christian has a life and world view that enables him to truly enjoy ordinary daily activities unlike the unbeliever, as the hymnwriter says:

> "Heaven above is softer blue;
> Earth around is sweeter green;
> Something lives in every hue,
> Christless eyes have never seen."

Further, there is no way to be "the salt of the earth and the light of the world" if the believer isolates himself from contact and interaction with the men of this world.

Third, this miracle teaches us something about *the importance of joy in life.* According to Psalm 104:15 and other passages, wine is a symbol of joy. Joy is a fruit of the Spirit (Gal. 5:22) and one of the three characteristics, with righteousness and peace, of the kingdom of God (Rom. 14:17). The Christian knows that true joy is derived from the Lord Jesus Christ. Only He can turn the tastelessness of daily life into something rich and robust and satisfying.

31

Typical Lesson

We may also learn something here from a symbolic and spiritual perspective. The lack of wine, the empty stone jars, and the abject mood at what should have been a festive occasion is an accurate picture of the state of the Jewish religion when Christ arrived on the scene. A. W. Pink has written, "Judaism still existed as a religious system, but it ministered no comfort to the heart. It had degenerated into a cold, mechanical routine, utterly destitute of joy in God. Israel had lost the joy of their espousals." By turning the water to wine, Jesus signifies his mission to establish a new covenant in place of the old.

The Motive behind the Miracle

John's summary statement in verse eleven reveals the motive behind this and every miracle our Lord would perform: "This beginning of miracles did Jesus in Cana of Galilee, and manifested forth his glory; and his disciples believed on him."

What was the purpose behind this and every miracle of Jesus? It was to "manifest forth his glory", i.e. to validate His identity as the Son of God and to give evidence that this Man was indeed more than a man.

The Beginning of Conflicts

There is another "beginning" in John 2, however. Not only does this chapter record the beginning of miracles, it also spotlights the beginning of conflicts.

John 2:12-17 is the first of several in John's Gospel to elaborate on the thought introduced in John 1:11: "*He came unto his own and his own received him not.*" This initial confrontation of religious apostasy will set the pace for the developing plot in John's Gospel.

Much of our Lord's earthly ministry consisted of face-to-face encounters with apostate Judaism. The Jewish people failed to recognize and receive Him as the anticipated Messiah simply because they had wandered so far from the truth that had been revealed to them. Many of them wanted a Messiah who would lead a political revolution against the Romans. They did not expect a Messiah who took issue with them. But Jesus was more concerned with religious, than political, apostasy.

"Will the real Jesus please stand up?" Just as Jesus upset the preconceived notions of people in his own day, the real Jesus challenges popular stereotypes today. Those who picture Jesus as a milk-toast, pacifistic hippie will have great difficulty reconciling that image with the courageous display of zeal for the glory of God he exhibits on this occasion.

Cleansing the Temple

Our Lord's first confrontation with religion run amok occurred in Jerusalem near the time of the Jewish Passover celebration (2:13). As he approached the temple courts, he witnessed a virtual market. People were transacting business —selling oxen, sheep and doves and processing the transaction at the point of sale (2:14).

It is easy to see how this situation had developed. The fact that the Law required the offering of sacrifices at Passover coupled with the other fact that many Jews had to travel a distance to Jerusalem for the feast was a situation ripe for an entrepreneurial solution. Some astute businessman saw an opportunity to, as it were, "kill two birds with one stone." He could make it more convenient for visitors to offer their sacrifice while making a little extra money on the side. After all, it couldn't be wrong (he must have reasoned) to profit a little when he was really providing a service to people who wanted to worship God.

The problem with this attempt to make worship more convenient, however, was that it quickly gained momentum. Before long, there were numerous merchants setting up shop in the temple courts themselves. One can imagine that even residents of Jerusalem might take advantage of the convenience of the situation. "Let's just buy our sacrifice on site today; that will save us a lot of hassle." One can also imagine that some who were not technically classified as "the poor" might still be tempted to save a little extra and instead of offering an ox or a sheep, might purchase the less expensive dove, a provision made by God for the poor and destitute, instead.

The bottom line is that this scene was really an object lesson of just how far the Jewish religion had strayed from God's revealed will. And drastic maladies call for drastic remedies. Witnessing the level to which the true worship of God had degenerated, Jesus fashioned a scourge of small cords and cleaned house. He drove these eager opportunists from the temple, turned over their tables, and poured out their money.

What motivated Jesus to take such a dramatic step? The explanation is given in verses 16-17: *"Take these things hence; make not my Father's house a house of merchandise. And his disciples remembered that it was written, The zeal of thine house hath eaten me up."* The Jews had made a business out of Divine worship. They had turned a place where prayer was wont to be made into a place of competitive trade and marketing schemes. If they had any initial scruples about it initially, I'm sure they justified it in their own minds—"We're providing a service; the end justifies the means". It wasn't long, however, until it became such a common practice to set up shop in the temple square that it no longer even occurred to them that they were making merchandise of the house of God.

To the people he challenged, then, Jesus' actions seemed to be an overreaction. They had compromised the pattern of true worship so far and for so long that they did not even recognize that they had strayed from God's word.

Did Jesus over-react? If the same kind of situation occurred today, would we think Jesus had handled the situation properly? Would we be tempted to think that he might have been a bit more tactful or diplomatic? Might it have been better if he had tried to talk to them first? Perhaps the emotional tension we feel toward this scene reveals the degree to which we have yet to learn what zeal for God's house and for the glory of God's name is all about. May zeal for God's glory and for the integrity of his house consume us, as well. And may such zeal prompt us to conviction and courage in His service.

Chapter 5
Dialogue with a Jewish Ruler (John 3)

John 3 records a lengthy conversation between Jesus and a Jewish ruler named Nicodemus. It was a conversation initiated by Nicodemus, who sought out Jesus, but directed by the Lord Jesus, who steered the topic of discussion from the outset.

One wonders if Nicodemus left Jesus' presence wondering precisely what had happened, for he scarcely offers his greeting before he finds himself engaged in a theological discussion with the One he admitted was a "teacher come from God". Whatever questions he intended to ask when he first arrived were soon forgotten.

We can be glad that our Lord engaged this powerful religious leader into a dialogue on two great themes: (1) The New Birth; (2) His Atoning Death on the Cross. By addressing these two themes, he highlights two primary flaws of Judaism. First, he exposes their preference for external form and religious ceremony in contrast to God's interest in the inward transformation of the heart by his Spirit. Secondly, he challenges the Jewish sense that they had a premium on the love of God by emphasizing God's love for "the world", i.e.

Gentiles as well as Jews. Both of these points must have surprised this Jewish, religious scholar, Nicodemus.

The New Birth

John 3:1-8 is a primer on the doctrine of regeneration. Jesus' intention, no doubt, is to emphasize the priority God places on the heart, though Jewish religion had degenerated into an emphasis on external rules, regulations, and ceremony.

The Source of the New Birth (v. 3)

The word "again" literally means "from above." Unlike one's first birth, which is a horizontal matter, Divine rebirth is a vertical matter. It comes "from above." What does that mean? It means that regeneration is supernatural, as opposed to natural, in origin. It is something miraculous and heavenly, not something commonplace and biological. Later in the conversation, Jesus said, *"We speak that we do know, and testify that we have seen, and ye receive not our witness. If I have told you earthly things and ye believe not* [that is, if I have illustrated spiritual truths in terms you are capable of understanding], *how shall ye believe if I tell you of heavenly things?"* (Jno. 3:11-12). Regeneration is a "heavenly thing," something supernatural, expressed in language that man can understand (i.e. the metaphor of birth) in order to communicate to man's finite mind. So, God is the source of the new birth.

Only God can regenerate. In the prologue to his gospel, John traced the origin of regeneration to God: *"But as many as received him, to them gave he power to become the sons of God, even to them that believe on his name: which were born, not of blood, nor of the will of the flesh, nor of the will of man, but of God"* (Jno. 1:12-13). The new birth is not the product of human lineage ("not of blood"), nor is it the result of a human relationship ("nor of the will of the flesh"), nor the result of a human decision ("nor of the will of man.") Man's will is not instrumental in his new birth. Man is born "of God" the preposition *of* denoting source or origin. People are not born again as a result of something they do, but solely on the basis of God's sovereign will and power.

The Nature of the New Birth (vs. 4-6)

Nicodemus was puzzled by the imagery. Notice his question. It is a question regarding the nature (that is, the kind) of this birth. Nicodemus was thinking in terms of the birth process (that which hospitals call "labor and delivery"), but Jesus used a word (Gr. *gennao*) that refers to the concept of generational descent.

In other words, Jesus focuses not on the experience of birth but on the fact that the father's nature is passed to his child. What happens in the new birth? What kind of birth is it? It is a birth in which the Divine nature is imparted to the soul. Your first birth, says Jesus, reproduced in you the nature of your parents: *"...that which is born of the flesh is flesh."* Your new birth, he concludes, implants within you the Divine nature: *"...and that which is born of the Spirit is spirit."* Just as children possess

39

the nature of the parents, God's children are given a new nature, a spiritual and Divine nature, when they are born again. This new nature is sinless and holy (1 Jno. 3:9). The thrust of the argument is clear: Regeneration is something supernatural. Only the Holy Spirit can affect a change of nature in the heart. That leads us to the next point.

The Necessity of the New Birth (v. 7)

Regeneration is necessary because people are by nature totally depraved. Without the new birth, no one will be saved. *Dei*, the Greek word translated "must," indicates logical necessity. By the use of such a strong term, Jesus indicates that regeneration is essential, imperative, and absolutely necessary for salvation. It is a vital link in the chain of sovereign grace. Some Bible students have erroneously concluded that because the word *dei* refers to logical necessity, it expresses the idea of human responsibility. In other words, they think that Jesus is suggesting that Nicodemus take personal responsibility for his own new birth. Notice however, that Jesus did not tell Nicodemus to *do* anything in order to be born again. He did not instruct him to make a decision or even to repent and believe the gospel. "Ye must be born again" is simply a statement of fact, not a command to be obeyed. It is a declarative, not an imperative, sentence. In fact, the words of the Lord Jesus, instead of suggesting that Nicodemus should assume personal responsibility for his own salvation, teach exactly the opposite idea.

The purpose of the entire passage might be summarized like this: *Regeneration is not something any man can do, for flesh can only produce flesh. It is a miraculous work of God's Spirit, who blows when and where He pleases.* Jesus is saying, "Yes, Nicodemus, the new birth is a necessity, but neither you nor any other man can cause it to happen, even if you could think of a way to return to the womb of your mother. Only God can perform this work."

Perhaps someone will object, "To tell a man about the necessity of being born again in one breath, then, that he is utterly helpless to produce such a work in his own soul in the next, is self-defeating and contradictory." On the contrary, our Lord's goal was to expose the fallacy of trusting in one's own efforts and works for salvation. If mere religiosity or devotion to a life of law-keeping could save a person, Nicodemus would have been safe. But, Jesus says, No one is safe, regardless of their achievements, family history, social status, or religious fervor. Because of the universality of sin, the new birth is necessary before anyone will see the face of God in peace. Further, because of sin's debilitating effect upon men, no one has the ability to rescue himself. John 3:7 does not teach that man must assume responsibility for his own salvation. It teaches rather that the sinner's only hope of eternal bliss is the sovereign grace of God.

There is another side to this truth about the necessity of regeneration. God, in His grace, has so arranged the work of salvation that everyone who was chosen in Christ before the foundation of the world will be called into new life at some point in their personal history. The new birth is sure and certain to all of the elect (Gal. 4:6; Rom. 8:28; 2 Tim. 1:9).

The Method of the New Birth (v. 8)

This verse addresses three important principles regarding the doctrine of the new birth. First, the verse teaches that *God is sovereign in regeneration* ("The wind bloweth where it listeth [pleases]..."). Just as the wind blows unrestrained by political, racial, geographical, or cultural obstacles, so the Spirit of God cannot be foiled or frustrated in His regenerating activity. No man can resist or handcuff the Spirit of God. No potential hurdle can thwart God's work of grace in the soul.

Secondly, the verse teaches that *regeneration is a Divine mystery* ("...cannot tell from whence it cometh and whither it goeth..."). It seems to be the rule that most people are unaware of the moment when the new birth occurred. Although many trace their new birth back to a certain date or time, such dates generally mark the moment when the person first understood the gospel or first committed himself to the Savior in gospel obedience. If so, the date to which the individual has attached significance as the date of regeneration is in fact the date of gospel conversion, a separate event entirely. To say that regeneration is a Divine mystery is to say that there is more to it than we can understand. Such mystery should prompt a spirit of reverential awe and worship from our hearts.

Thirdly, the text teaches that *everyone who is born again is born again in precisely the same way* ("...so is every one that is born of the Spirit..."). Arminianism requires a separate method of saving sinners in different circumstances. For example, it requires one method to save the unevangelized heathen, another to save the infant that dies in infancy, another to save the mentally retarded, another to save the individual who lived prior to the Law, another to save the one who lived under the Mosaic Law, and another to save the person who lives on this side of the cross.

Salvation by God's sovereign grace through the direct work of the Holy Spirit upon the heart is a method of salvation that will reach the infant, the infidel, the heathen, the mentally deficient, the Old Testament Jew, and the individual who has all the privileges of New Testament Christianity available to him. All who are born again are quickened in precisely the same way, by the sovereign and mysterious operation of the Holy Spirit within the soul.

So what is the method by which men are born again? It is nothing more or less than the sovereign and direct work of the Holy Spirit. Regeneration is immediate. God does not use the works of the sinner, on the one hand, nor the efforts of the gospel preacher, on the other hand, as either the basis or the method for imparting life to the soul. Faith is the gift of God in regeneration (Eph. 2:8). What does that mean? It means that the sinner responds to the life giving voice of the Lord Jesus Christ (Jno. 5:25) like Lazarus responded to the command of

Jesus in John 11. It is an involuntary response, below the level of consciousness, a perfect obedience to the Divine imperative of Jesus. The Lord God is the active cause; the sinner is the passive recipient. This is irresistible grace! The gift of faith enables the newborn soul to function in the spiritual realm, an ability he did not have prior to his quickening (Jno. 3:3b,5b; I Cor. 2:14). It also gives the individual the ability to believe, or, if you please, "ears to hear" (Rev. 2:7,11; Pro. 20:12; Mt. 11:15). The gospel is, subsequently, addressed to the regenerate (Acts 2:39; Acts 13:16, 26), for the unregenerate cannot believe (Jno. 8:43; Jno. 10:26; Rom. 3:10-18).

The Brazen Serpent (John 3:9-15)

After the conversation on the great truth of regeneration, Nicodemus still expresses confusion: "How can these things be?" (v. 9). Jesus responds that a "master in Israel" like Nicodemus, schooled in the teaching of the Old Testament, should know these things (v. 10). The Savior's reply indicates that the doctrine of the new birth is not a strictly New Testament revelation, but a truth taught in the Old Testament as well (cf. Eze. 36:26-27; Jer. 32:29).

Then the Lord Jesus makes two statements that are nothing short of claims to deity: "We speak that we do know, and testify that we have seen" (v. 11); "No man hath ascended up to heaven, but he that came down from heaven, even the Son of man which is in heaven" (v. 13).

Verse eleven indicates that Jesus was not merely engaging in philosophical speculation, but expressing spiritual realities of which he had first-hand, immediate knowledge. The only way this could be true is if he was, in fact, the Son of God.

Verse thirteen indicates that Christ's native residence was heaven. To "ascend" to heaven is not the same as "entering" into heaven, for the disembodied souls of many saints had certainly entered into heaven upon their respective physical deaths (cf. 2 Cor. 5:6). Further, Elijah "went up by a whirlwind into heaven" (2 Kings 2:11). But only Christ can ascend into heaven, a concept that means "to go up under one's own power."[1] The text further describes the omnipresence of the Lord Jesus Christ, an attribute belonging to God: "...*even the Son of man that is in heaven.*"

In verse 14, Jesus directs attention to his impending death by crucifixion. The juxtaposition of this passage concerning the cross of Christ with the foregoing discussion of the blessing of regeneration reveals a profound theological truth, namely, that the work of regeneration in the heart is founded

---

[1]The Ascension of the Lord Jesus Christ is as essential to an orthodox Christology as the Incarnation, Crucifixion and Resurrection of Christ. Ascension means that Jesus has been exalted to the Father's right hand, the highest position in the universe where He has been invested with supreme honor and authority. In Ephesians 4:8-16, a passage based on Psalm 68:18, the ascension of Christ is described in terms of the public celebration of a returning military hero. This event is also associated with the coronation of a king in Daniel 7, Philippians 2:9-11, Ephesians 1:20-23, and Acts 2:34-36. This image from the ancient world in which a new king would proceed to the throne to be crowned in an elaborate procession, take his seat upon the throne and begin his reign at the royal court by distributing gifts to his servants and appointing governors over the realm captures the substance of this thrilling truth.

and predicated on the atoning death of Christ on the cross. Regenerating grace, in other words, is inseparably connected to justifying grace. The apostle Paul makes this very connection in Titus 3:5-7. The point is unmistakable: *All for whom Christ died on the cross will be personally and vitally quickened into new life at some point between conception and death.* The legal work of salvation wrought out by Jesus Christ on the cross will be vitally applied to each individual heir of grace.

Christ now draws a comparison between a familiar historical event–the brazen serpent lifted atop a pole in Numbers 21–and the lifting up of the Lord Jesus Christ on the cross. The parallels between these two events are very revealing. Perhaps a brief recap of that episode would be helpful.

Israel was under Divine judgment for murmuring against the Lord. God sent fiery serpents among the people which bit them so that some had even died. Others were suffering from the venomous snake bites. When the people cried out in repentance, God instructed Moses to make a serpent of brass and to put it on a pole. When those who were bitten looked upon the brazen serpent, they were healed. From this story we may glean the following insights.

1. *The remedy necessary to deliver men from the poison of sin would be provided by God.* Just as God provided the remedy

to the fatal venom of the fiery serpents, so God provided the remedy to the fatal poison of sin.

2. *The One who solves the problem of sin would share the same nature with the one who caused the offense.* Serpents bit the people and a serpent would heal them. Even so, *"by man came death, and by man also came the resurrection of the dead. For as in Adam all die, even so in Christ shall all be made alive"* (1 Cor. 15:21-22).

3. *The One who remedies the sin problem would possess two natures.* Brass is an alloy, consisting of copper and zinc, a corruptible and an incorruptible metal. So the Lord Jesus Christ would possess two natures – a human nature that was subject to death and a Divine nature that could never die.

4. *The prescribed remedy was only intended for the children of Israel.* This was not a remedy to every man, woman, boy and girl who would ever be snake bitten, but rather to the covenant people of God. Even so, the lifting up of Christ on the cross was for the benefit of spiritual Israel, the covenant family of God.

5. *Healing from the deadly venom was promised only to those who looked upon the serpent.* Even so, those who look by faith on Christ crucified, as he is proclaimed in the gospel, find healing from a convicted conscience. *"Look unto me and be ye saved all the ends of the earth"* is the gracious appeal of the gospel (Is. 45:22). Those who look upon Him in believing

47

faith give evidence that they are in possession of eternal life (Jno. 3:15).

A. W. Pink makes the powerful point that they were not told to manufacture some ointment for their wounds, or to minister to others who were wounded in order to find relief for their own wounds, or to fight the serpents, or to make an offering to the serpent on the pole, or to pray to the serpent, or to look at Moses, or to look at their wounds. They were told to look upon the brazen serpent. Only a believing gaze upon Christ crucified will bring deliverance to the sin-sick soul.

Promises to the Believer (John 3:16)

The conversation with Nicodemus began with a discussion of the new birth and proceeded to a discussion of the benefits of believing on Christ crucified. This sequence of birth before belief is one of the major motifs of John's Gospel, appearing again and again in its pages (cf. 1:12-13).

John 3:16 is arguably the most beloved verse in the entire Bible. I suspect, however, that it is also one of the most misunderstood verses in the entire Bible.

Many quote the verse to prove "general atonement," the idea that Christ died for all men without exception, and "decisional regeneration," the idea that the only thing necessary to make the death of Christ effective is the sinner's act of putting his/her faith in the Savior.

But John 3:16 is not talking about believing in order to be born again at all, for the new birth precedes belief, as we have previously noted. Neither is the text suggesting that God loved and Christ made salvation possible for every human being, indiscriminately. The text, in other words, is not a prescription for salvation if the sinner will but believe, but a promise to the believer that he will never perish. Note first,

The Motive of the Cross

"*God so loved...*" It was love that motivated redemption. This mysterious, Divine love, as other scriptures teach us, was according to the sovereign purpose of God (1 Jno. 4:9-10) and in spite of legitimate demerit in those on whom it was bestowed (Rom. 5:6-8).

The monosyllable "so" indicates that the magnitude of this love is immeasurable by finite minds. Packed into that little term "so" is the height, breadth, depth, and length of that love expressed by Paul in Ephesians 3.

That love was manifested or proved by the greatest gift that has ever been given – "*...that He gave His only begotten Son...*". The love of God was not simply a static emotion. He demonstrated that love by giving His everything. It was love that sent the Son of God into the world and love that nailed Him to the cruel cross. Nothing short of love delivered up the Lord of Glory on behalf of sinful men. There is no greater display of the wondrous love of God than the cross of Christ. Note further,

The Objects of that Love

"God so loved the world..." That the word "world" in John's Gospel seldom means every man, woman, boy and girl that has lived, lives now, or will live in the future, is not difficult to establish. In fact, the word "world" is used in three different ways in the very next verse: "For God sent not his Son into the *world* [that is, physical creation] to condemn the *world* [that is, to judge humanity] but that the *world* [that is, God's elect] through Him might be saved" (v. 17). Just as we define the word "world" by the context in everyday conversation, i.e. the sports world, the political world, the world of fashion, etc., so the word must be defined by its context when used in Scripture.

Obviously the idea that John 3:16 means that God loved, and Christ died on behalf of, every human being indiscriminately contradicts passages such as Romans 9:11-13 and Matthew 7:23. The "world" of John 3:16 is the world of God's elect, the world to whom God will not impute iniquity (cf. 2 Cor. 5:18). Consider John 17:9 where Christ distinguishes those for whom He makes intercession from "the world" at large, and 1 John 5:18 where a distinction is made between the "we" who are "of God" while the "whole world" lies in wickedness, as further proofs of the importance of interpreting this term by its context.

In particular terms, it is important to remember that Jesus is discussing God's love with a Jewish ruler and the Jews believed that they had a corner on the love of God. By employing the word "world" in John 3:16, Jesus expands the objects of God's love beyond the Jews only, and teaches this Jewish ruler that God has a people for whom Christ would die not only from the Jews but also from the Gentiles. Note finally,

The Promise to the Believer

John 3:16 is simply a statement of fact—a declarative, not an imperative, sentence. It is not an instruction or a command. Jesus simply states that the person who believes (present tense) will not perish. Instead, the believer has (present tense) everlasting life. Belief in Christ, then, is not a condition for eternal salvation, but an evidence of such. Show me someone who believes in the Lord Jesus Christ and I will show you someone whom God loved and Christ redeemed.

Condemnation (John 3:17-21)

The gift of God's only begotten Son to the world that He loved is the blessed theme of this familiar portion of Scripture. Never has a more sublime theme been recorded.

Verses 17-21 answer the question "Why did God send his Son into the world? For what purpose did Christ come?" The answer can be only one of two possible options: Either (1) Christ came to judge sinners; or (2) Christ came to save sinners. The New Testament epistles teach that one day He is coming to judge the world, cf. Acts 17:31; 2 Ths. 1:7-9, but that particular function is associated with the second, not the initial, coming of Christ. He came the first time, however, "not to condemn the world, but that the world through him might be saved" (3:17).

Salvation and condemnation are antithetical (or opposite) concepts. Those Christ saved are not condemned (Rom. 8:1, 34). Those for whom He did not die, on the other hand, are under condemnation.

This passage analyzes the reason salvation was necessary. It was necessary that Christ come into the world to save sinners because all men by nature are under condemnation. All would be finally judged and sentenced to eternal fire had God not sent His Son into the world to save the objects of His love.

The word "might" in verse 17 does not indicate any uncertainty or doubt. To interpret the phrase as if it means that some "might be" and some "might not be saved" is to read into the text something that it does not say. In fact, the term as employed by the Holy Spirit here conveys the meaning of "should"[2] and expresses the thought that Christ himself is the means or instrument by which this salvation from final ruin was accomplished.

Believers are not Condemned (v. 18a)

We learned in verse 16 that those who believe in the Lord Jesus Christ give evidence that they have been born again (cf.

---

[2] Just as it does in 1 Peter 3:18.

52

3:3-8) and, consequently, are eternally secure. Now in verse 18, we learn the further truth that belief in Christ is also an evidence of a justified state: "He that believeth on him is not condemned."

The act of believing is not the means of escaping condemnation, for the previous verse insists that Christ himself is that means (i.e. "...that the world *through Him* might be saved" – v. 17b). But belief in Christ is an evidence that such a person has been rescued from the wrath of God.

The Nature of Condemnation (vs. 18b-21)

What is the nature of this "condemnation" from which the Son of God saved those that he loved? Verses 18b-21 answer that question.

First, condemnation (i.e. the natural state of man from which Christ came to save His people and for which sinners will finally be judged by God) consists of **unbelief**. The reason we can say categorically that the believer gives evidence of grace is because men are by nature unbelievers: "*...But he that believeth not is condemned already...*"

Notice those two words "condemned already." Man by nature is an unbeliever because he is already condemned. Man dead in trespasses and sins cannot believe (Jno. 8:43; cf. 1 Cor. 2:14). Those who are not of His "sheep" do not believe in the Lord Jesus Christ (Jno. 10:26). Only the born-again child of God is capable of believing in Christ. Hence, just as belief is an evidence by which we know that a person is not condemned, unbelief is an evidence by which we know that someone is "condemned already." In other words, the unbeliever gives evidence of a native sinfulness that merits Divine wrath. Of course, this is the condition of all men by nature—we are all "children of wrath even as others" (Eph. 2:3). Left in that wretched condition, the sinner will eventually suffer the judgment of God—that is to say, he is condemned already.

Secondly, condemnation consists of *a predisposition toward and preference for darkness*: "*And this is the condemnation, that light is come into the world, and men loved darkness rather than light, because their deeds were evil*" (v. 19). Apart from grace, no man loves what is good, what is true, or what is right. The natural man is predisposed and bent toward sin. In fact, he loves it, prefers it, and will always choose it when faced with an opportunity.

This verse exposes the radical effects of total depravity. Every facet of the natural man's composition is fallen. His mind, will, affections, and deeds are antithetical to truth and holiness. Left in this natural state and bereft of intervening grace, he will most certainly suffer eternal punishment, for the natural man is under condemnation. His nature is not disposed to believe in or turn to the Lord Jesus Christ. His only hope is salvation by grace alone.

Chapter 6
John the Baptist's Witness (John 3:22-36)

Following his conversation with Nicodemus, Jesus and his disciples journeyed to Salim near the place where John was baptizing and the disciples of Jesus also began to baptize (cf. 4:2). At this, some of John's disciples expressed concern that Jesus was intruding on John's territory and threatening his popularity. John was losing his crowd to Jesus. How would he respond to his dwindling popularity?

Learning to Think like a Servant (John 3:22-30)

John's response exhibits genuine humility and a true servant's spirit. A close examination of his reply may teach us how to think like a servant.

Promotion Comes From God

First, a servant mentality arises from the understanding that lasting success and advance is not something man can manufacture. *"A man can receive* [margin "take unto himself"] *nothing, except it be given him from heaven"* (v. 27). John is repeating the same principle the Psalmist taught in Psalm 75:5-7: *"Lift not up your horn on high...for promotion cometh neither from the east, nor from the west, nor from the south. But God is the judge: he putteth down one, and setteth up another."*

John's philosophy of ministry is based on the premise that a man's specific field of labor and extent of influence is God's gift, not a personal right. The church is His church, not mine, and it is His sovereign right to use me, or not use me as the case may be, as He sees fit. Such a reminder is the first step to cultivating a servant's spirit.

No Illusions of Grandeur

Next, John says, "*Ye yourselves bear me witness, that I said, I am not the Christ, but that I am sent before him*" (v. 28). His words suggest that a servant is someone who maintains an accurate self-assessment and possesses no illusions of grandeur.

Romans 12:3 exhorts Christians not to think more highly of themselves than they ought, but to think soberly, according as God has dealt to every man the measure of faith. John never pretended to be indispensable in God's kingdom. He reminds his disciples that he had told them from the outset that he occupied a subservient and temporary role and was content to do so. It is when men mistake their position for personal importance and assume popularity as a personal right that they feel jealous of the success of another.

A humble person knows his own limitations. He doesn't exaggerate his own importance but remembers that he is an expendable item and that the cause of Christ is more important than personal notoriety. John models such a humble attitude.

Finding Joy in the Master

Third, John explains that a true servant finds fulfillment and satisfaction when his Master is the glorified: "*He that hath the bride is the bridegroom: but the friend of the bridegroom, which standeth and heareth him, rejoiceth greatly because of the bridegroom's voice: this my joy therefore is fulfilled"* (v. 29).

A true servant of Christ is content to divert all attention toward the Lord Jesus, just as the best man at a wedding directs all attention to the bridegroom. Like Abraham's servant, he wants to draw attention only to his Master (cf. Gen. 24:35). Christ is the bridegroom and believers are His bride. John, and every true gospel servant, finds his greatest satisfaction in the glory of Christ. With the 18th Century Englishman Henry Martyn, a servant-hearted minister will say, "I do not think I could endure existence if Christ were not glorified."

Self-Effacement

Finally, a servant is committed to Christ's popularity above his own: *"He must increase, but I must decrease"* (v. 30). John thinks of his ministry in terms of the fading light of the moon as the sun outshines it. Every true servant is committed to the principle in Colossians 1:16: *"In all things, He must have the preeminence."* A servant who is content to occupy a position of anonymity in order to facilitate the greater glory of his Master is eminently useful in the kingdom of God. May the tribe of such men increase.

The Superiority of Jesus Christ (John 3:31-36)

In verses 31-36, John the Baptist continues his final public testimony to the Lord Jesus Christ by highlighting several areas in which Christ was superior to himself.

His Origin (v. 31)

First, John affirms that Christ came *"from above and is above all"* —a statement he explains in the next breath, *"he that cometh from heaven is above all."* In contrast, John is *"of the earth,"* meaning that he is nothing more than a man. Language attesting to the Divine nature of the Lord Jesus Christ and the fact that He was indeed more than a man—for He is the God-man—could not be any clearer.

This earth was not our Lord's home. He did not begin to exist here, but existed from all eternity, visiting the earth from his home in heaven. How many times John will repeat this theme! *"I came down from heaven..."* (6:38); *"No man hath ascended up to heaven, but He that came down from heaven..."* (3:13); *"The bread of God is He which cometh down from heaven..."* (6:33); *"I am the living bread which came down from heaven..."* (6:51); *"I came forth from the Father, and am come into the world..."* (16:28).

Like John, every believer is of the earth (cf. 1 Cor. 15:47-48). Our understanding and vision and abilities are finite and limited. But Christ has infinite ability, perfect and omniscient understanding.

Since Christ is *"from above,"* He is necessarily *"above all,"* i.e., sovereign. In all things He possesses preeminence. None is higher or greater or superior to Him. Such claims can only legitimately be made of God Himself.

His Testimony (vs. 32-34a)

Next, John emphasizes that the testimony of the Lord Jesus was firsthand, eyewitness testimony: *"And what he hath seen and heard, that he testifieth...for He whom God hath sent speaketh the words of God"* (vs. 32a, 34a). Unlike John and the prophets before him, Jesus did not preach and teach by revelation of the Holy Spirit. He spoke with immediate, firsthand knowledge of the very heavenly realities that He had witnessed.

Compared to the masses of humanity, however, the preaching and teaching of Jesus Christ met with small success: "...*and no man receiveth his testimony.*" Obviously, this does not mean that no one at all attended the ministry of Christ, for the next verse speaks of those "*that received his testimony.*" But John is simply reiterating one of the dominant motifs in this Gospel record, namely that some believed and received the message and that others believed not and received Him not. Compared to the nation of Israel as a whole, few received Christ's testimony. His true followers remain a minority among men unto this day.

Why do many refuse to receive His testimony? As previously explained in 3:19, they love darkness rather than light because their deeds are evil. It is because of their native depravity that men prefer darkness to light. Left in that natural state, man can only expect the "*wrath of God*" (v. 36).

The believer, on the contrary, "*hath set to his seal* [that is, has certified and ratified] *that God is true*" and gives evidence that he is in possession of "*everlasting life*" (vs. 33, 36). God is a reality to the believer, not an abstract concept or philosophical idea.

The Measure of the Spirit (v. 34b)

Further, John attests to the superiority of Christ in terms of the fact that the Holy Spirit attended His ministry in full measure. Others, like John, had the Spirit "by measure." They understood but fragments of the truth and proclaimed but

59

bits and pieces of it. The presence of the Spirit on their labors varied. But the Lord Jesus Christ had complete knowledge of the truth of God for He is "the Truth" (cf. Jno. 14:6). When the Holy Spirit came upon Him at His baptism, He "abode" with Him (Jno. 1:32). Hence, Christ could say, "*The Spirit of the Lord is upon me, because He hath anointed me to preach the gospel to the poor...*" (Lk. 4:18). He was "*anointed with the oil of gladness above His fellows*" (Heb. 1:9). Unlike his preachers, Christ possessed not merely one or two gifts of the Spirit, but every spiritual gift. Truly, the "*fullness of the Godhead*" dwelt bodily in our Lord Jesus Christ" (Col. 2:9).

His Sonship (v. 35)

Finally, John affirms as proof of Christ's superiority His Sonship: "*The Father loveth the Son and hath given all things into His hand.*" John himself was one of God's servants, but Christ was His Son. He was not simply one of many messengers or prophets, but the Beloved Son, co-essential and co-equal with the Father.

Chapter 7
Dialogue with a Samaritan Woman (John 4)

O ur Lord's journey from Judea back to Galilee took him through Samaria. It was at Sychar, a particular city of Samaria, that he stopped to rest at Jacob's well. Here Jesus encountered a Samaritan woman whose spiritual needs exceeded her physical needs.

The International Scope of the Gospel

This is the second lengthy conversation between Jesus and an individual recorded in John's Gospel. The first was with a Jewish ruler named Nicodemus. He was a man of prominence and sophistication—a religious leader among the Jews. This one, however, is much less conventional and much more potentially scandalous.

First it is a conversation in public with a woman. In his book *How Christianity Changed the World*, Alvin Schmidt comments that modern Western people may not view the humane and respectful way Jesus interacted with the Samaritan woman as unusual; nevertheless, it directly challenged rabbinic law prohibiting a man from speaking to a woman in public and the prevailing view that viewed women as inferior beings. He writes, "The rabbinic oral law was quite explicit: 'He who talks with a woman [in public] brings evil upon himself' (*Aboth* 1.5). Another rabbinic teaching prominent in Jesus' day taught, 'One is not so much as to greet a woman' (*Berakhoth* 43b)."[1]

Secondly, the conversation was unusual because this woman was a Samaritan. The Jews viewed the Samaritans, ethnic hybrids, as inferiors. The woman herself admits the profound contempt for between Jews and Samaritans in the statement, "*...for the Jews have no dealings with the Samaritans*" (v. 9b).

These two facts, i.e. that she was a woman and that she was a Samaritan, form the basis for both the woman's and the disciples' surprise that Jesus would speak with her (cf. vs. 9, 27). But this episode not only illustrates our Lord's refusal to adapt to conventional norms but a further, very profound truth—namely, a truth regarding the international scope of gospel blessings.

God has a people out of every nation and kindred and tongue (Rev. 5:9). In Christ, former racial, class, and gender distinctions no longer matter (Gal. 3:28). He came to bring the good news to His people, whether they were Jews or Samaritans, male or female, in fulfillment of the promise of the Abrahamic Covenant: "*In thee and in thy seed shall **all the families of the earth** be blessed.*" The coming of the Messiah was not a blessing restricted to the natural descendants of

---

[1] Alvin Schmidt, *How Christianity Changed the World*, p. 103.

Abraham, but a gift of grace to every elect, whatever his/her ethnic or social status might be.

The late James Montgomery Boice contrasts these two encounters in John's *Gospel*: "It is difficult to imagine a greater contrast between two persons than the contrast between the important and sophisticated Nicodemus, this ruler of the Jews, and the simple Samaritan woman. He was a Jew; she was a Samaritan. He was a Pharisee; she belonged to no religious party. He was a politician; she had no status whatsoever. He was a scholar; she was uneducated. He was highly moral; she was immoral. He had a name; she is nameless. He was a man; she was a woman. He came at night, to protect his reputation; she, who had no reputation, came at noon. Nicodemus came seeking; the woman was sought by Jesus."[2]

It is indeed a great contrast. But the point is that both have the same spiritual need that only Christ can meet. Nicodemus teaches that none is too high and important to be above the need for Christ. The Samaritan woman teaches that none is too lowly and insignificant to be below the reach of Christ.

The differences between these two notwithstanding, Nicodemus and the Samaritan woman are also very similar. They had a number of things in common.

First, both were personally unaware of their spiritual need. Each thought they were spiritually well. He was self-satisfied and content in his fastidious observance of the law, and she in

---

[2] James M. Boice, *The Gospel of John* (Vol. 1), p. 272.

her superstitious tradition of worshiping at the temple of Manasseh on Mt. Gerizim, like her ancestors (v. 20). Neither imagined that they needed something beyond a sheer external or formal religiosity.

Second, both had difficulty grasping the spiritual message of Jesus. He interpreted the Lord's discussion of the "new birth" and she the Savior's discussion of "living water" in very human and physical terms. Each processed thought only in the context of the five natural senses and failed to grasp by faith the good news Jesus proclaimed.

Third, and most importantly, both felt an inner hunger for and need of something—they just didn't know what. This sense of need is an indication that both were children of God, for only the child of God seeks the things of the Spirit (cf. 1 Cor. 2:14; Acts 17:27). What each needed, only Christ could supply. Only He can give "living water" to refresh the deepest needs of the soul.

Living Water

I never cease to marvel at Christ's ability to use whatever common imagery that was at his disposal as an illustration of spiritual truth. On this occasion, he employs the familiar human experience of seeking satisfaction from a drink of water as an occasion to teach a lesson regarding the source of spiritual satisfaction: *"Whosoever drinketh of this water shall thirst again: but whosoever drinketh of the water that I shall give him shall never thirst; but the water that I shall give him shall be in him a well of water springing up into everlasting life"* (vs. 13-14).

A Doctrinal Lesson

Obviously, the Lord Jesus is speaking in terms of spiritual experience. He is describing the refreshing and reviving influence of the Holy Spirit in the believer's inner man as he lives each day. This "living water" is something that can be obtained in answer to prayer—by asking (v. 10). Behind every subjective personal experience, however, stands an objective doctrinal truth.

The doctrinal truth behind this promise is that only the person who is in possession of spiritual life will experience spiritual thirst. Even in nature's realm, dead men do not get thirsty. The dead have no appetite, no sensation of thirst, no desire for refreshment. Show me a person who desires spiritual refreshment—someone who has a spiritual thirst— and I'll show you someone who already has spiritual life.

A Familiar Image

Living water? In putting a spiritual spin on the need for water, Christ echoes a familiar Old Testament image. Time and again in the Old Testament, the benefit of drinking water to satisfy physical needs is given a spiritual connotation: *"Therefore with joy shall ye draw water out of the wells of salvation"* (Is. 12:3); *"For I will pour water on him that is thirsty, and floods upon the dry ground: I will pour my spirit upon thy seed, and my blessing upon thine offspring"* (Is. 44:3); *"My people have committed two evils; they have forsaken me the fountain of living waters, and hewed them out cisterns, broken cisterns, that can hold no water"* (Jer. 2:13); *"For with thee is the fountain of life..."* (Ps. 36:9); *"Ho, everyone that thirsteth, come ye to the waters, and he that hath no money; come ye, buy, and eat; yea, come, buy wine and milk without money and without price"* (Is. 55:1).

Further, in Jewish speech, living water meant water that was flowing, like water from a spring or an artesian well, in contrast to water that was static and potentially stagnant.

This Jewish habit of using water to represent spiritual refreshment is continued even after the personal ministry of the Lord Jesus Christ. In Revelation 22:1, the apostle John writes, *"And he showed me a pure river of water of life, clear as crystal, proceeding out of the throne of God and of the Lamb."*[3]

Experiential Lessons

What, then, is Jesus saying in regard to this living water? What principles might we deduce?

First, these words affirm that **only the Lord can satisfy the deepest needs of the soul.** The benefit of earthly solutions to soul needs is only temporary – *"Whosoever drinketh of this water shall thirst again..."* True satisfaction can only come from Christ. He alone can quench the appetite of the one who "hungers and thirsts for righteousness." All earthly pleasures are temporary and fading. Christ alone can give lasting

---

[3] See also Rev. 7:17

66

satisfaction. That the Psalmist knew this fact is evident: *"My soul thirsteth for God, for the living God..."* (Ps. 42:2); *"O God... my soul thirsteth for thee, my flesh longeth for thee in a dry and thirsty land, where no water is"* (Ps. 63:1).

Secondly, **the Lord Jesus is just as essential to the sustenance of our souls as water is to the sustenance of our bodies**. Unless we draw refreshment from him on a daily basis, we risk spiritual dehydration and the complete shut-down of all spiritual systems.

Thirdly, Christ's reference to a *"well of water in you springing up into everlasting life"* suggests a yet further truth: **refreshment comes from within—from an internal supply— not from external activity**. It is a peace and joy passing all understanding that Christ is describing—a soul rest—a heart happiness—an inward renewal. When Paul prays for the Ephesians that they *"might be strengthened with might by his Spirit in the inner man and that Christ would dwell in their hearts by faith,"* he is describing the reality Christ here highlights to this woman.

Finally, notice the "vertical" reference, i.e. *"springing up."* It is interesting to note that when Jesus revisits the theme of "living water" in John 7, he will focus on the horizontal impact of these inward resources – *"...out of his belly shall flow rivers of living water"* (7:38). The internal fountain that springs from the heart of a believer who is filled with the Holy Spirit equips him both for worship and communion with God (vertically) and service and ministry toward his fellow man

67

(horizontally). How crucial it is, therefore, that we avail ourselves of this living water and drink deeply from this fountain in our daily Christian experience!

Getting Personal (4:15-18)

This intriguing dialogue about the abstract subject of "living water" suddenly takes a very personal turn: "*The woman saith unto him, Sir give me this water, that I thirst not, neither come hither to draw. Jesus saith unto her, Go call thy husband and come hither. The woman answered and said, I have no husband. Jesus said unto her, Thou hast well said, I have no husband: for thou hast had five husbands; and he whom thou now hast is not thy husband: in that saidst thou truly.*"

This single sentence from Jesus must have jolted the Samaritan woman like a blow in the solar plexus. At once, she is brought face to face with her past failure and her present guilt. Prior to this point, she has been content to discuss obtuse theological points with this intriguing stranger, but suddenly she feels very uncomfortable. He has gotten personal. Somehow he knows everything about her and she knows that he knows.

Until a person recognizes his/her own sin and deep guilt—until, that is, religion gets personal—the gospel will make very little, if any, impact on his/her life. Faith will be merely an intellectual or notional matter. But when the Holy Spirit convicts of sin so that an individual becomes a sensible sinner —when He speaks that dreadful sentence "Thou art the man" and it strikes like an arrow of conviction in the heart—then the gospel of grace is welcome news.

We call this experience—when a sinner comes face to face with the truth about himself and subsequently is enabled to personally appropriate the message that Christ Jesus is the Savior of sinners—"gospel conversion." This person can now say, "The Lord is *my* shepherd" and "He loved *me* and gave himself for *me*".

"Come see a man that told me all things that ever I did: is not this the Christ?" (4:29), the Samaritan woman later reported. Our Lord is "the heart knower" (Jno. 2:24-25; 1 Sam. 16:7; Acts 1:24; Rev. 2:23). All things are exposed and open to His eyes (Heb. 4:13). He knew all about this woman, and He knows all about you and me. No detail of our lives is withheld from Him.

Getting personal, then, is basic and fundamental to conversion. Until a person is brought face to face with their own failure and need, that person will never truly recognize their own spiritual need. The Lord works first to wound, then to heal; first to kill, then to make alive; first to expose the need, then to reveal the remedy.

Salvation is of the Jews (4:19-26)

The confrontational nature of this discussion takes another turn. The uncomfortable woman attempts to change the subject and to shift the spotlight off herself by introducing a point of debate: *"Our fathers worshiped in this mountain; and ye say, that in Jerusalem is the place where men ought to worship"* (4:20).

Perhaps a brief historical review will be helpful in understanding the argument. When the northern kingdom of Israel fell to the Assyrians in 722 B.C., the Assyrians moved settlers into Samaria from various cities (cf. 2 Kings 17). Meanwhile, some Jewish people who had escaped captivity remained and intermarried with the newcomers, producing a race that was one-half Jewish and one-half Assyrian. To Jews in the southern kingdom of Judah, the northerners had lost their identity.

A little over a century later, the southern kingdom would be carried into Babylonian captivity for 70 years. When they returned and set out to rebuild the temple in 445 B.C., the Samaritans offered to help them but were refused (cf. Ezra 4). The spurned Samaritans decided to build their own temple on Mt. Gerizim—a gift from Sanballat (the infamous opponent of Nehemiah's rebuilding project) to his son-in-law Manasseh—and thus a rival religion was formed.

It was this temple and this religion to which the woman referred. Jesus answered her, first, by saying *"Salvation is of the Jews."* It is important to note that he is not claiming racial or ethnic superiority, but affirming in no uncertain terms that all religions are not created equal. To many modern people, Jesus' answer appears intolerable. "Who has the right to say that one religion is right and another is wrong?" But Jesus would not allow the Samaritan woman to believe that a religion of human origin could be acceptable to the revealed worship of Jehovah.

The oracles of God had been committed to the Jewish people (Rom. 3:1). All religions are not equally plausible and valid. In fact, according to the Bible, every other religion apart from that which God has revealed in His word is an idolatrous religion. There is such a thing as "true worship," aside from which every other form of worship is false.

True Worship

It is common to hear someone suggest that it doesn't matter who or how you worship, as long as you worship something. But God is interested in "true" worship. In fact, as the Lord Jesus tells the Samaritan woman, the Father is searching for true worshipers (Jno. 4:23b; cf. 2 Chr. 16:9; Is. 66:1-2; Eze. 34:11-12, 16-22).

The New Testament church exists to promote, as its primary goal and objective, the practice of true worship (Eph. 3:20). The church is not in the business of populating heaven. Instead, her primary function is to find God's children who have been born of His Spirit and teach them how to worship and serve the God who saved them.

That means, necessarily, that true worship is something subsequent to regeneration. Every one of the elect will be quickened, but every elect may not be a true worshiper. In fact it is possible for a born again child of God to fall short of the goal of true worship. The Bible teaches that some of them may engage in "vain worship," that is, simply the form of worship (Mt. 15:9). Others may engage in "ignorant worship," that is, worship that is not informed by Divine revelation (Acts 17:22), and still others in "will worship," i.e. worship from faulty motives (Col. 2:23).

What then is "true worship"? Jesus teaches the Samaritan woman that there are three non-negotiables of true worship.

Worship the Father

First, a true worshiper understands that God alone is a worthy object of worship: *"The hour cometh and now is when the true worshippers shall **worship the Father**..."* (v. 23). Worship is His exclusive right. Every other object of worship beside the true and living God is an idol (1 Jno. 5:20-21; Col. 3:5). The church at Thessalonica began to practice true worship when they *"turned to God from idols"* (1 Ths. 1:9).

Someone once said that you can tell who your god is by answering the following questions: What dominates your thought-life? What controls your time? On what do you spend your money? What is it that you feel you could not live without?

Even though we love people, we must never let another person become a god to us. Even though we appreciate our jobs, we must not allow a job to define our lives. Even though it is not wrong to enjoy a hobby, it should never be permitted to consume our energy and time. A true worshiper is someone who understands that he can continue living even if he lost a number of these things, but he could not continue to exist without the Lord.

Worship in Spirit

Secondly, true worship involves worshiping *"in spirit"* (v. 24). This may refer to our dependence on the Holy Spirit for true worship to occur (Phi. 3:3; 1 Cor. 2:4; 1 Pet. 1:12). However, it likely speaks of the fact that true worship is something that is spiritual and not merely formal. It is something that must come from within—from the heart—not simply something external and ritualistic.

The Samaritan woman thought worship was something geographical (v. 20). But true worship is not a matter of place or geography. Neither is it a matter of posture, or of ceremony. The heart must be involved for true worship to occur (cf. Lam. 3:40-41; Mt. 15:8; Eph. 3:17).

It is possible, however, for a person to emphasize this aspect to the exclusion of the next. In such cases, worship turns into a kind of religious free-for-all where emotion predominates. Another component is, therefore, essential.

Worship in Truth

The Lord Jesus teaches that true worship involves not only inflamed hearts, but also informed minds. Doctrine is as essential to true worship as delight; correct content is as necessary as proper motives.

It is not enough to simply be sincere or to approach God with a heart full of love. Truth, i.e. orthodoxy or doctrinal correctness, is also essential. Likewise, it is not enough to be doctrinally correct if our hearts are cold and formal.

Worship in truth means that our worship is consistent with God's revealed word (Acts 17:23; Rom. 10:1-3). True worship is worship that is informed by and according to the fundamentals of Christian doctrine concerning the character of God, the person and work of Christ, and the doctrines of grace. The doctrinal content exhibited in the worship of the redeemed in Revelation 5:8-9 is an illustration of worshiping in truth.

This dual dynamic—spirit and truth—is vital and fundamental to the practice of true worship.

Come, See a Man (John 4:25-30, 39-42)

The Lord's encounter with the Samaritan woman is an account of *conversion*. Here is an individual whose thinking was confused and whose life was misdirected. Step by step, as Jesus reminds her of her spiritual needs (vs. 10-14), exposes the broken relationships in her past and sinful circumstances of her present living arrangement (vs. 16-18), and challenges her to think about the subject of worship in more personal and spiritual terms (vs. 20-24), He prepares her for a revelation of His identity as the promised Messiah.

This Samaritan woman is not unlike people today. She is so preconditioned to think in physical terms that she is slow to grasp the spiritual (vs. 11, 15). She is uncomfortable with the personal focus on her life and attempts to change the subject to a more comfortable abstract subject (v. 19). Now, in verse 25, she attempts to postpone making a commitment by saying, *"I know that Messiah cometh...and when he is come, he will tell us all things."* She is focused on the physical, uncomfortable with the personal, and hesitant to admit the inevitable. "Some day when the Messiah comes," she procrastinates, "we will know the truth."

Jesus' response to the woman restores reality: *"I that speak unto thee am* **he**" (v. 26). The italicized word "he" was added by the English translators to preserve the sense of the Greek text. What Jesus actually said to the woman was, "I am."

Obviously, the Lord is claiming to be the anticipated Messiah. In common vernacular, he replies to her, "You're talking to him right now." But more than that, Jesus claims the premier Old Testament name for God, i.e. *Jehovah,* as His own. *"I am that I am"* was the name God revealed to Moses at the burning bush. That the Lord Jesus now claims equality with Jehovah by employing the sacred name as his own is incontrovertible. In fact, this is one of seven occasions in John's Gospel where the Lord Jesus assumes the title "I am" (cf. 6:20; 8:24, 28, 58; 13:19; 18:5). Further, there are seven more occasions where the name is coupled with a noun to indicate that He is the One who supplies our every need (6:35; 8:12; 10:9; 10:11; 11:25; 14:6; 15:1).

Did the Samaritan woman understand that Jesus was claiming to be God? We don't really know the extent of her familiarity with this most sacred of names for God. What we do know is that this sentence pushed her off the fence of ambivalence and brought about a change in her life.

A Change of Values

"The woman then left her waterpot and went into the city, and saith to the men..." (v. 28). She came to the well that day thinking only about her physical need for water. Now, that need has faded into such insignificance that she abandons the waterpot and leaves it sitting on the well. What is important to her has changed. Her priorities have been altered. Another object has now captured her attention.

A Change in Confidence

"...Come see a man which told me all things that ever I did: is not this the Christ?" (v. 29). No longer does she halt between two opinions. Ambivalence has given way to a confident and courageous confession of Christ. She now believes. The evidence is overwhelming. "He knows too much about me," she admits, "to be anything less than the Messiah." She has been converted.

On any other occasion, the men of Sychar would have paid little attention to the testimony of this woman. But there is something about the personal testimony of a true believer that is convincing. *"Then they went out of the city and came unto him"*

(v. 30). The woman did not stop with the men. She told others. Her encounter with Christ was the topic of conversation whomever she met: *"And many of the Samaritans of that city believed on him for the saying of the woman, which testified, He told me all that ever I did"* (v. 39).

How important it is to learn from this Samaritan woman what it means to give witness to the Lord Jesus Christ! "Come, see a man" was her gospel appeal. That sentence alone conveys the essence of our gospel message. The sole, great attraction of the Church is expressed in this invitation: *"Come, see a Man!"*

The men of Sychar asked Jesus to abide with them and he spent two more days preaching and teaching the people of that city (v. 40). *"And many more believed because of His own word; and said unto the woman, Now we believe, not because of thy saying: for we have heard him ourselves, and know that this is indeed the Christ, the Savior of the world"* (vs. 41-42). How much good may be done by a single, genuine conversion!

Serving God – An Urgent Priority (John 4:31-38)

John 4:31-38 is a parenthetical passage inserted into the narrative of Christ's encounter with the Samaritan woman to reveal what happened in the interim between her departure and the effect of her testimony on the people of Sychar. *"In the mean while, his disciples prayed him saying, Master, eat"* (v. 31).

The passage records a conversation between Jesus and his disciples. They had earlier left him sitting on the well while

77

they had gone to find something to eat. They knew that he was weary, but now, he seemed refreshed. They implored him to eat the food they had brought, but he replied, *"I have meat to eat that ye know not of"* (v. 32).

Like the Samaritan woman, they have difficulty understanding the spiritual connotation of his words. They are thinking in purely material and physical terms: *"Therefore said the disciples one to another, Hath any man brought him aught to eat?"* (v. 33). But he is speaking of spiritual, not physical, refreshment and satisfaction. He had been invigorated and strengthened not by natural bread, but by serving the Father in speaking to this woman.

The Priority of Serving God

He explains in verse 34: *"My meat is to do the will of Him that sent me and to finish His work."* The principle taught in this verse concerns the priority of serving God. Christ valued "doing the will" of the Father even above his physical needs. He found satisfaction in serving God that superseded his natural hunger.

The disciples needed to learn this lesson, i.e. that personal privation and hardship may indeed be necessary in serving the Lord, for they would be called upon to give up various comforts and privileges in the course of following Christ. Paul, for example, suffered great personal discomfort as he outlines in 2 Corinthians 11:23-28. But like his Lord before him, Paul not only learned to be content in every condition

(Phi. 4:11-13), but found true fulfillment in living for Christ (Phi. 1:21).

This was the *"meat they knew not of"* (v. 32). And though many believers express a desire to do the will of God, yet rare is the Christian who doesn't look for a loop-hole when God's will runs counter to his own. It is only when a person surrenders his will entirely to the Lord, saying "Thy way, not mine, O Lord," and commits himself to doing the will of God in every situation, come what may, that he will know and experience the kind of spiritual fulfillment Jesus here describes.

Church history is replete with examples of God sustaining His servants when they esteemed the words of His mouth more than their necessary food and put His kingdom before their own personal needs (cf. Job 23:12; Jno. 6:27). The world scoffs at such apparent irresponsibility, but doing the will of the Father and laboring in His cause and kingdom is bread that strengthens man's heart. Jesus lived to serve His Father and to do the Father's will (Jno. 6:38; Heb. 10:7), not to satisfy himself or fulfill his own physical needs. May His followers take their cue from Him and learn the true satisfaction and fulfillment that likewise comes from serving the Lord.

The Urgency of Serving God

Because serving the Lord is so important, it calls for a special sense of urgency: *"Say not ye, There are yet four months and then cometh the harvest? Behold I say unto you, Lift up your eyes and look on the fields; for they are white already to harvest"* (v. 35).

The Lord Jesus warns his disciples about the tendency to procrastinate. Don't succumb to the temptation, he urges, to pace yourself—to save something for a rainy day—to conserve your energy for some hypothetical future occasion. Get to work now; there is work to be done now; the window of opportunity is open now, so run through it.

This, too, is an important lesson. No one knows how much time they have left in this world. It won't be long before the evil day of old age and feebleness will impair your faculties and prevent you from serving with the same energy that you now possess. The harvest is ready to be gathered now. There are people around you who need the wisdom and insight that God has given you. There are sheep aplenty who need to hear about the Good Shepherd who laid down his own life for them. Now is the accepted time; today is the day of salvation.

Whether you sow the seed or reap the harvest in serving your Lord, you are participating in a quality of life (i.e. *"life eternal"* v. 36) that is its own ample reward: *"And he that reapeth receiveth wages and gathereth fruit unto life eternal: that both he that soweth and he that reapeth may rejoice together"* (v. 36). There is no better compensation than that enjoyed by those who labor in the vineyard of the Lord Jesus Christ. A life of service to God is indeed the best life of all.

Chapter 8
Miracles Two and Three (John 4:34 – 5:9)

After spending time in the city of Sychar, Jesus resumed his journey for his home country of Galilee. Though his earlier visit there had been less than enjoyable, evoking the proverb that "a prophet hath no honor in his own country" (v. 44; cf. Lk. 4:14-30; Mr. 6:1-6), he had nonetheless determined not to give up but to try again. This time, *"the Galilaeans received him, having seen all the things that he did at Jerusalem at the feast: for they also went to the feast"* (v. 45).

Healing the Nobleman's Son

As news spread that Jesus was once again in Cana of Galilee, a nobleman who lived about twenty-five miles away —a four hour journey—made the trip to Cana (vs. 46-47). The Greek word translated "nobleman" (*basilikos*) indicates that this man was considered to be royalty. Perhaps he was one of King Herod's court officials, or some kind of petty king himself. At any rate, he was a man of considerable public importance and rank. Remembering how Jesus had made the water into wine during his previous visit (v. 46; cf. 2:1-12), the nobleman sought Jesus out on behalf of his son who was gravely ill.

We may learn from this account that social status and privilege does not exempt one from pain and suffering. James Montgomery Boice has written,

"It does not matter who you may be, sooner or later you are going to experience great sorrows or even tragedies in life. You may be rich or poor, a man or a woman, black or white. Tragedy inevitably will become a part of your personal experience and there will be nothing you can do to avoid it...Psychologists tell us that life begins with pain, as the child, who for the first nine months of its life has rested warmly and comfortably within the uterus of its mother, is suddenly pushed and pulled into a hostile environment in which his first independent act is to cry. The experience is akin to strangulation as the baby gasps for its life. For a time after birth the mother cares for the baby's needs. Yet, as the child grows up, the years progressively knock away the props of life and the child is forced increasingly to depend on his own resources. He must learn to eat and clothe himself. Eventually he must go to school, then earn a living. In time there will be the failure of his plans and the dissolution of cherished relationships. There will be pain and sickness. Death will inevitably come to friends and family, and at last the person himself will face his own death…"[1]

The nobleman's initial request for Jesus to accompany him back to Capernaum to heal his son was met with what might have been interpreted as a rebuke from Jesus: *"Then said Jesus unto him, Except ye see signs and wonders, ye will not believe"* (v. 48). Perhaps this was primarily intended as an indictment on the "curiosity seekers" who were present, but it was also a test of the nobleman's sincerity and faith. Would this man of stature be offended by "the carpenter's son"? Instead, the nobleman exhibited a truly noble spiritual quality, i.e. humility. He simply replied by reiterating his request, *"Sir, come down ere my child die"* (v. 49).

I suggest that Jesus had another motive for his apparent rebuke. He wanted to teach the lesson that he is sovereign over distance. He does not have to be physically present to work miracles. Faith involves trusting the Lord to work in whatever way he chooses, whether we witness it personally or not. Seeing is not believing, but the very opposite is true— believing is seeing! The nobleman needed to believe first, then he would see.

Jesus said, *"Go thy way; thy son liveth."* And the nobleman *"believed the word that Jesus had spoken and went his way"* (v. 50). On his way home, the nobleman's servants met him and told him that the boy was alive and had rallied. When he inquired

---

[1] James M. Boice, *The Gospel of John (Vol. 1)*, p. 342.

at what time the boy began to improve, they said, "*Yesterday at the seventh hour the fever left him. So the father knew that it was at the same hour in the which Jesus said unto him, Thy son liveth: and himself believed and his whole house*" (vs. 50-53).

John cites the healing of the nobleman's son as "*the second miracle that Jesus did*" (v. 54), that is, the second of the seven signs referenced in John's Gospel as evidence for the Deity of Jesus Christ. The first miracle, at the wedding feast, demonstrated that Jesus is sovereign over the elements of nature. The second, proves that He is sovereign over distance. He is not limited in his power by the typical boundaries and restrictions that limit ordinary people. Jesus manifested forth his glory (that is, his divine nature) and the nobleman and his whole house became converts.

Christ at Bethesda (John 5:1-9)

John 5 begins with an account of the third of seven miracles cited by John as evidence for the deity of Jesus. Like the miracle at the wedding feast in Cana, this account of the healing of the impotent man is exclusive to John's *Gospel*.

The narrative does not specifically state which "feast of the Jews" was under way when Jesus returned to Jerusalem, but it was probably the feast of Pentecost. The feast of Passover is mentioned in John 2:13 and Pentecost was fifty days after Passover. It was one of the three annual feasts in which the law required every Jewish male to go to Jerusalem for its observance (cf. Deut. 16).

It was at this feast that our Lord encountered a very pathetic scene at the pool of Bethesda, which had five porches: *"In these lay a great multitude of impotent folk, of blind, halt, withered, waiting for the moving of the water"* (v. 3). Whether or not the description in verse four is factual or a legend among the Jews is not clear, but it appears that this particular pool, at least seasonally, had medicinal properties, perhaps like some of the hot or mineral springs in Arkansas and Texas. The phenomenon was so brief, however, that only the first one in received any benefit.

What a pathetic scene indeed! All of these crippled, paralyzed, and otherwise handicapped people, lying in the porches near this pool, *"waiting for the moving of the water"* is enough to move the most insensitive to pity. One particular man was there who had suffered an infirmity for thirty-eight years (v. 5). We are not told specifically what kind of disease it was but evidently it had something to do with his mobility, for he required a friend to help him into the water (v. 7).

The misery of the impotent man's condition is compounded by the fact that he had no friend. When Jesus asked him *"Wilt thou be made whole?"* the man replied, *"Sir, I have no man...to put me in the water, but while I am coming, another steppeth down before me."*

The impotent man, however, did, in fact, have a man – the man Christ Jesus! He had an omnipotent man. He had a friend in Jesus who could cure apparently incurable diseases

—who could help the helpless—who could remedy every malady. What a friend we have in Jesus!

Jesus commanded the man, *"Rise, take up thy bed and walk"* (v. 8). This is a remarkable command, for the man had been in this condition for almost four decades. But when the Lord issues a command, he also supplies the strength necessary to obey it. May we learn from this that our business is to follow His commands, regardless of how enfeebled and impotent we may feel to be. His grace will be sufficient for us.

The impotent man was immediately healed (v. 9). Unlike those who happened to step first into the healing waters and begin to mend gradually, the crippled man was instantly cured.

This miracle occurred on *"the Sabbath"* (v. 9), the mention of which leads into the first hint in John's *Gospel* concerning the intense conflict that would ensue between the religious leaders and the Lord Jesus, culminating in his crucifixion and death.

Chapter 9
Christology According to Jesus (John 5)

*C*hristology is a theological term that refers to the study of the person and work of Christ. John 5 is one of the Christological gems, a veritable gold-mine of material relative to this sublime theme, in the New Testament. Of course, who better to teach Christology than the Lord Jesus Christ himself?

Jesus Christ is Lord of the Sabbath (Jno. 5:10-18)

Each passage in John's Gospel is an expansion and embellishment of a principle found in the Prologue, i.e. the first eighteen verses of chapter one. This particular passage in John 5 expands on the principle found in John 1:11: *"He came unto his own and his own received him not."*

Here the opposition to Jesus takes the form not only of rejection, but also of active hostility. Twice we read that *"the Jews sought to kill"* Jesus (vs. 16, 18).

The explanation at the end of the account of the healing at the Pool of Bethesda, i.e. *"...and on the same day was the Sabbath"* (v. 9), prepares us for the conflict now revealed in verses 10-18. It is likely that the Jewish leaders had watched Jesus closely since the episode with the money-changers in the temple (cf. John 2). But this is the first "hard evidence" they were able to gather against him.

How was this evidence gathered? The impotent man, now "cured" and "made whole" (notice that Jesus did not merely offer therapy or some form of assistance, but wrought an actual cure and healing of the man) was seen carrying his bed on the Sabbath. When he was accused of breaching rabbinical law concerning the Sabbath, the man reported that his Healer had told him to "take up his bed and walk".

A. W. Pink observes, "Christ was not ignorant of the current teaching about the Sabbath, and He knew full well what would be the consequences should this healed man carry his bed on the Sabbath day. But he had come to set His people free from the shackles which religious zealots had forged."[1] It is important to note that Jesus never breached God's commandments, though he often challenged the amendments that men had added to God's Law and the traditional conventions of man-made religion and society.

This gives us a clue into the real complaint the Jewish religious leaders had with Jesus. It wasn't so much that He had breached the Sabbath. Their antipathy toward Jesus was due to his refusal to play by their rules. The religious leaders saw Jesus as a maverick and a rebel. They could not control him, and that fact incensed them.

The restrictions and prohibitions imposed on the Sabbath day by the rabbis, however, had the effect of making a god

---

[1] Arthur W. Pink, *Exposition of the Gospel of John*, p. 251.

out of the "law." On another occasion, Jesus reminded his detractors that *"the Sabbath was made for man, not man for the Sabbath"* (Mr. 2:27). In other words, man was not created in order to serve the Sabbath. The Sabbath was established for man's benefit. By making a god out of the Sabbath, the Jewish leaders had imposed an unnecessary burden on the people.

Jesus refused to keep their rules simply to avoid conflict. A peace purchased by compromise of principle invariably costs the person who made the compromise his integrity, and those who will be affected by the compromise, their comfort and safety. Submission to the religious leaders for the sake of maintaining peace would necessarily mean continued oppression of the common people. Jesus came to liberate the captives from the bondage of legalism—to set His people free from the grievous burdens imposed on them by man. Because He is the One who invented the Sabbath, He is Lord of the Sabbath. He rules it, in other words, not the other way around. The religious leaders had perverted it, but now, it would be restored to its original intention – a day of rest from affliction, burdens, and toil.

Christ's Seven-Fold Equality with the Father
(Jno. 5:17-31)

"My Father worketh hitherto, and I work" (5:17). When he made this statement, Jesus meant that he would continue the work that God the Father had performed prior to that point. The Jews rightly understood this to be a claim to equality with

God, or deity, and accused Jesus of blasphemy. Hence, Jesus responded by highlighting seven particular areas in which he is coequal with the Father.

(1) **Deeds** – *"The Son can do nothing of himself, but what he seeth the Father do: for what things soever he doeth, these also doeth the Son likewise..."* (vs.19-20). The things that Jesus does are identical to the things the Father does. Did God create? So did Jesus (cf. Jno. 1:3; Col. 1:16; Heb. 1:2). Did God heal lepers? So did Jesus (cf. Mr. 1:40). The wonderful works of God that we read about in the Old Testament (Ps. 111:4) are duplicated in the activities of the Lord Jesus Christ recorded in the four Gospels.

(2) **Quickening** – *"For as the Father raiseth up the dead, and quickeneth them; even so the Son quickeneth whom he will"* (v. 21). Christ is equal to the Father in terms of his life-giving work. Just as God restored life to the Shunammite woman's son (2 Kings 4), so the Lord Jesus restored life to Jairus' daughter, the widow of Nain's son, and Lazarus (cf. Lk. 7, Lk. 8, Jno. 11). Furthermore, he quickens his elect in the inner man when he speaks the life-giving voice and they live (5:25; cf. 1 Cor. 15:45).

(3) **Judgment** – *"For the Father judgeth no man, but hath committed all judgment unto the Son"* (v. 22). Thirdly, Christ is equal to the Father in his authority. In the same way that a family business might be transferred from father to son, so the government of the universe has

90

been turned over to the Lord Jesus Christ. The Lamb now inhabits the throne, as the book of Revelation describes. Christ now reigns as Sovereign Lord and King (see also v. 27).

(4) **Honor** – *"That all men should honor the Son, even as they honor the Father..."* (v. 23). Fourthly, the Son shares the right of worship with the Father. The very honor that men owe to God is owed to the Lord Jesus Christ, for he is God of very God. One of the ways we honor the Son is by *"hearing his word and believing on him"*, as verse 24 indicates. Of course, this passage reiterates the important doctrinal principle that has been emphasized several times already in John's *Gospel*, namely that regeneration must precede gospel conversion. The person that "hears" and "believes" already has everlasting life, according to the verb tenses in verse 24. How did he come into possession of eternal life? Verse 25 answers that he was given everlasting life by an effectual and immediate and irresistible, Divine call.

(5) **Life** – *"For as the Father hath life in himself; so hath he given to the Son to have life in himself"* (v. 26). In the fifth place, Christ is equal to the Father in terms of his resurrecting power. Not only did Jesus raise some who were physically dead back to physical life during his public ministry; and not only does Jesus raise his elect people who are dead in trespasses and in sins to spiritual life in Him; but one day, He will speak to the

cemeteries and raise the bodies that have been long since laid to rest, some to everlasting life and others to everlasting condemnation and death (vs. 28-29). Jesus Christ will be the agent of the general resurrection and final judgment at the last day.

(6) **Will** – "*...I seek not mine own will, but the will of the Father which hath sent me*" (v. 30). Next, Christ will is in perfect harmony and unity with the Father. His design and objectives are not different or distinct from the Father's. He seeks the very same goals that the Father seeks. His mind and the Father's are one.

(7) **Witness** – "*If I bear witness of myself, my witness is not true. There is another that beareth witness of me; and I know that the witness which He witnesseth of me is true*" (vs. 31-32). Finally, Christ's testimony that He is the Son of God (cf. vs. 17-18) is consistent with the testimony that God the Father gave to the Lored Jesus at his baptism and at the Mount of Transfiguration. There the Father identified Jesus as His "beloved Son".

In seven ways, therefore, Jesus highlights his co-equality and unity with God the Father. Those who claim that Jesus never suggested that he was God need to closely examine this passage. The Jews that heard these words did not fail to get the message. They fully grasped the case that Jesus presented as a claim to Deity, and sought to kill him for it.

Five Witnesses of Christ's Divine Authority
(Jno. 5:31-46)

On the heels of this seven-fold defense of His deity, Christ offers five witnesses of His divine authority. These five witnesses testify to the same fact, namely, that Jesus of Nazareth is indeed God.

It is common for skeptics and non-believers to argue that Jesus never claimed to be God. That such an argument is specious may be proved by John 8:13-16, John 10:30, and a number of other passages. On this occasion, however, the Lord acquiesces to the argument of his opponents. They argued that just because he might claim to be equal with God does not make it true. So Jesus concedes the point. He spots his detractors a point in the debate and says, "*If I bear witness of myself, my witness is not true*" (v. 31). He means, "If I am independently claiming equality with God, then you might be justified to say that the claim is merely a personal opinion."

But lest they think that his case for equality with the Father is nothing more than a personal delusion of grandeur, Jesus summons five witnesses to testify of his Divine authority.

(1) **The Father** – "*There is another that beareth witness of me; and I know that the witness which he witnesseth of me is true...the Father himself which hath sent me hath borne witness of me...*" (vs. 32, 37)

When did the Father bear witness to the Son's true identity? He did so at the Savior's baptism (Mt. 3:17), and again at the Mount of Transfiguration (Lk. 9:35).

(2) **John the Baptist** – *"Ye sent unto John, and bare witness unto the truth. But I receive not testimony from man: but these things I say, that ye might be saved..."* (vs. 33-35).

Even though the Lord Jesus did not need John the Baptist's testimony to validate His identity as the Messiah, He cited the fact of John's endorsement on this occasion because the people considered John a true prophet. So Jesus reminds them that they had inquired of John concerning His identity and John had told them in no uncertain terms that Jesus was the Lamb of God, the promised and anticipated Messiah.

(3) **His Miracles** – *"But I have greater witness than that of John: for the works which the Father hath given me to finish, the same works that I do, bear witness of me, that the Father hath sent me"* (v. 36). Christ gave sight to the blind, speech to the dumb, the capacity to hear to the deaf, peace to the demon-possessed, and cleansing to the lepers. He raised the dead to life, walked the waves of Galilee, turned the water to wine, calmed the storm at sea, and fed multitudes with a few loaves and fish. These miracles furnish proof positive of His divine nature.

The miracles Jesus performed were unique and distinct from other supposed miracle-workers in several ways: (1) Their sheer *number* – He did not perform only one or two, but many miracles; (2) Their *visibility* – He did not perform miracles in secret, but in open day and before many witnesses, healing infirmities that might be easily verified; (3) Their *character* – He did no miracle to impress people with His ability, but to show mercy and compassion to the sufferer; (4) Their *spontaneity* – There was nothing staged or prescripted about the miracles Christ performed. Instead, they took place during the ordinary course of His ministry; (5) Their *efficacy* – There was never a single failure.

(4) **The Scriptures** – *"Search the scriptures; for in them ye think ye have eternal life: and they are they which testify of me"* (v. 39). Fourthly, our Lord cites the Old Testament as a witness to His Divine authority. The Messianic prophecies of the Old Testament predicted with surprising detail and specificity the birth, life, death, and resurrection of the Lord Jesus Christ.

(5) **Moses** – *"For had ye believed Moses, ye would have believed me: for he wrote of me"* (v. 46) The fifth and final witness he cites is Moses. Moses' Law pointed forward to and found fulfillment in Him (cf. Lk. 24:27). Each of the sacrifices under the old Law anticipated His perfect sacrifice on Calvary.

In spite of these many witnesses, Jesus' auditors would not be convinced. He indicts them over and again in this passage: "...*ye have not his word abiding in you*" (v. 38); "*Ye will not come unto me*" (v. 40); "...*ye have not the love of God in you*" (v. 42); "...*ye receive me not*" (v. 43); "...*ye seek not the honor that cometh from God only*" (v. 44); "...*ye believe not [Moses'] writings*" (v. 47).

This stunning indictment exposes the very character of unbelief. Unbelief, in its most grotesque form, is a sin that refuses to acknowledge the evidence because of a proud attachment to preconceived notions. Jesus has given ample proofs and evidences for his deity in this chapter, but his opponents still wanted to kill him. Such is the corruption that indwells the human heart by nature.

Chapter 10
Jesus and the Multitudes (John 6:1-33)

John 6 opens with the narratives of two further miracles of Jesus. Miracles number four and five are cited to give two more proofs to John's purpose statement in 20:31: "...*these are written that ye may believe that Jesus Christ is the Son of God.*"

The result of these miracles, however, was that the crowd following Jesus increased significantly. He knows that a large majority of these "new converts" are actuated by faulty motives and sets out to winnow the spurious chaff from the genuine wheat.

The Fourth Miracle (Jno. 6:1-15)

The passage before us records the fourth miracle in this "book of the seven signs." It is the feeding of the five thousand. Unlike some of the miracles that are exclusive to John's *Gospel*, this one is referenced in each of the other Gospel accounts (cf. Mt. 14:13-21; Mr. 6:30-44; Lk. 9:10-17). It is the only miracle Jesus performed that is recorded in each of the Gospel records.

The feeding of the multitude was a very public miracle. Over five thousand people witnessed it and participated in it.

Not only did they see the transformation of five barley loaves and two small fish into a meal sufficient for five thousand with twelve baskets of fragments remaining, but they also personally experienced it by partaking in the meal.

This miracle demonstrates the Deity of Jesus Christ by showing His sovereignty over difficulties[1]. It occurred shortly before the annual Feast of Passover (v. 4)[2] and great crowds had assembled around Jesus, hoping to witness other miracles (v. 2). The Passover Feast reminded the Jews of the night when their ancestors had feasted on the paschal lamb. In John 6, Jesus, the Lamb of God, both provides bread for the people and testifies that he is himself the food of God's people.

As the multitude approached the Lord and his disciples, Jesus asked Philip, *"Whence shall we buy bread, that these may eat?"* (v. 5). He asked the question to test Philip, not to gather information for himself, *"for he himself knew what he would do"* (v. 6).

Like Philip, we are frequently confronted in daily life with trying and difficult situations."How will we resolve this problem?" we ask ourselves. Usually, we approach the difficulty like Philip did by looking at the resources at our disposal—thinking only in terms of our physical circumstances. Like Philip, again, we fail to turn in faith to the Lord.

---

[1] The previous miracles demonstrated His sovereignty over Disability, Distance, and Disease, respectively.

[2] This detail is crucial to the interpretation of John 6. The entire chapter is interpreted in the light of this Passover Feast.

Philip responded, "*Two hundred pennyworth of bread is not sufficient for them, that every one of them may take a little*" (v. 7). His words echo the enormity of the difficulty they faced. He must have had a mathematical mind, for Philip instantly computes how much money would be necessary to feed such a multitude. Two hundred pennyworth is approximately seven months worth of wages. Jesus had actually asked "where" they might find enough bread for such a multitude ("*whence*" —v. 5), but Philip is preoccupied with "how" they might come up with enough money for such a crowd. The point is clear: *Jesus does not want us to worry about the means of resolving difficult circumstances, but to think about the source of our help.*

Andrew joins the conversation with a suggestion, but admits that it would not really be a solution to the problem: "*There is a lad here which hath five barley loaves and two small fishes: but what are they among so many?*" (v. 9). Neither of these disciples has factored Omnipotence into this equation. Both have made their calculations without consideration of the Christ in their midst. I'm sure every reader is very familiar with this kind of unbelief, for we too forget about the promises of Omnipotence to his children.

Jesus replied, "*Make the men sit down*" (v. 10). A. W. Pink's comment on this verse is noteworthy: "How thankful we should be that God's blessings are dispensed according to the riches of His grace, and not according to the poverty of our faith."[3] Though circumstances were not conducive to the command, yet the disciples obeyed the directive.

When Jesus had given thanks he gave the loaves to the disciples and they distributed them to the multitude. A supernatural miracle occurred and everyone ate as much as he or she wanted, with twelve baskets of fragments left over. Such is the power of the Lord Jesus Christ.

The Fifth Miracle (Jno. 6:16-24)

On the heels of the feeding of the multitude, Jesus performed yet another miracle: *"And when even was now come, his disciples went down unto the sea. And entered into a ship"* (vs. 16-17a). The fifth miracle in this "book of the seven signs"— i.e. Jesus walking on the water—demonstrates Jesus' sovereignty over creation and the elements of nature.

Matthew's account of this miracle explains that Jesus sent his disciples ahead and the multitudes away (Mt. 14:22). It is evident that Jesus wanted a time of solitude. It is also likely that he intends to teach his disciples an important lesson.

What lesson did he intend to teach them? Mark's account gives us a clue: *"For they considered not the miracle of the loaves"* (Mr. 6:52). The faltering and flagging faith of the disciples on this stormy occasion at sea demonstrates just how quickly we tend to forget past deliverances. And the lesson our Lord intends to teach on this occasion is the importance of using past deliverances as a strength to faith in present trials.

---

[3] Arthur W. Pink, *Exposition of the Gospel of John*, p. 293.

A Test of Faith

It is by means of testing that faith is strengthened. On this occasion, the test took the form of darkness, loneliness, and adversity. The disciples found themselves alone at sea as darkness fell. Suddenly, in typical form for the sea of Galilee, a great storm unexpectedly arose (vs. 17-18).

How typical is this of the believer's experience! Our journey through this world is marked by unanticipated storms. We find ourselves alone in the darkness, and wonder why the Master tarries while the tempest rages.

What did the disciples do? Did they simply give up in despair? No, they attempted to "row" themselves out of difficulty (v. 19). How important it is for the believer who is in the midst of a storm to keep going and not to simply lie down in surrender! Though the disciples in the midst of the storm may have thought that the Lord was oblivious to or unconcerned with their plight, Jesus was praying while they were struggling. Even now as we struggle to keep going in the midst of the storm, our Great High Priest is making intercession for us. When you continue rowing, therefore, the Lord will come, in His own good time, and deliver you.

A Display of Glory

"So when they had rowed about five and twenty or thirty furlongs,[4] *they see Jesus walking on the sea, and drawing nigh unto*

---

[4] A furlong is approximately 600 ft, or 1/8 of a mile. Twenty-five furlongs, then, would be a little over three miles.

the ship: and they were afraid" (v. 19). Notice that the Lord Jesus is not at the mercy of physical elements. He is not limited in His power or restricted in His ability by this material world. Like the other miracles, this sign displays the Divine nature of Christ. It shows that He is God of very God. As the One who created all matter, Jesus Christ is not controlled or limited by the world that He made.

The disciples responded to this unusual sight in fear. They failed to remember the miracle of the loaves. To those of mature faith, however, His sovereignty is not threatening, but reassuring evidence that He is able to overcome every obstacle.

Though the disciples falter in fear, the Lord Jesus demonstrates mercy: *"It is I; be not afraid"* (v. 20). How blessed it is that He knows our frame and remembers we are dust! Upon this revelation, the disciples *"willingly received him into the ship"* (v. 21). With Christ in the vessel, we may smile at the storm.

The miracle, however, does not end here: *"...and immediately the ship was at the land whither they went"* (v. 21b). Note the word "immediately." The Lord Jesus Christ is sovereign not only over matter (i.e. walking on the water), but also time and space (i.e. "immediately the ship was at land"). Truly, this is the Son of God!

Three Questions (Jno. 6:25-33)

When the multitude caught up with Jesus, they asked him three questions. The Lord Jesus answered their questions as he frequently answered other inquiries, i.e. by ignoring superficialities and cutting right to the heart of the matter.

When Did You Come Here?

First, they asked *"Whence camest thou hither?"* (v. 25). It is a question admitting their perplexity at his apparent disappearance. We might expect Jesus to answer directly: "Oh, I'm sorry, I came over to the other side of the sea last night to regroup and spend some necessary time alone with the Father." Instead he ignores the superficialities of protocol and "cuts to the chase" to expose their insincere motives: *"Verily, verily, I say unto you, Ye seek me, not because ye saw the miracles, but because ye did eat of the loaves, and were filled"* (v. 26).

Our Lord knows the hearts of all men. This occasion was no exception. He knew that his sudden popularity was due not to genuine interest in his message, but a desire for personal comfort and satisfaction. How many people today frequent "churches" with similar motives?

Jesus counsels the "free lunch" disciples to distinguish between physical (or material) and spiritual benefits: *"Labor not for the meat which perisheth, but for that meat which endureth unto everlasting life, which the Son of man shall give unto you: for him hath God the Father sealed"* (v. 27). How much energy is expended in this world for physical gratification! And how frequently do people forget the principle that man does not live by bread alone, but by every word that proceeds from the mouth of God! (Mt. 4:4; cf. Is. 55:2).

What Can We Do to Serve God?

The second question they asked him was, *"What shall we do, that we might work the works of God?"* (v. 28). They understood that he had just exposed their faulty motives. They must have felt a bit embarrassed that he knew their interests were primarily physical and selfish. So they said, "Give us some advice on what we might do to serve and please God. We want to do something for Him."

Our Lord responds, *"This is the work of God, that ye believe on him whom he hath sent"* (v. 29). His reply might be expressed in these terms: "So, you want to do something for God? The best thing you can do is to believe on me." Again, he "cuts through the fluff" of insincerity and gets to the heart of the issue. The most basic and fundamental way to please and serve God is by means of believing in the Lord Jesus Christ.

Don't miss the important theological point in this verse, i.e. **believing in Jesus is a work.** Now of course, faith itself, i.e. the ability to believe, is a gift of Divine grace (cf. Eph. 2:8). Until a person is born again, therefore, he does not possess the capacity to believe. But the act of believing in Jesus Christ as the Son of God and embracing the gospel message is a work.

The following syllogism might be deduced from this fact:

1. Since the Scripture is very clear about the fact that eternal salvation is not of, by, or according to our works (Eph. 2:9; Titus 3:5; 2 Tim. 1:9);
2. And since believing in Jesus Christ is a work;
3. Then, eternal salvation is not conditioned on the act of believing in Christ.

What role, then, does the act of believing in the Lord Jesus Christ play? It is an evidence of, not a condition to, eternal salvation. People do not believe the gospel in order to be born again but because they have been given the grace of faith and the ability to believe in regeneration. Believing in Jesus, however, is a work that is necessary to pleasing and serving God in this life. That is precisely the point that Jesus makes.

What Proof Do You Have That You Are the Messiah?

Finally, they ask *"What sign showest thou then, that we may see, and believe thee, what doest thou work?"* (v. 30). They understood that Jesus is claiming that God sent him, but they admit that their skepticism will not be removed unless He gives them a sign. They argue that the "fathers" were given a sign that validated Moses' identity: *"Our fathers did eat manna in the desert..."* (v. 31). Jesus replies *"Moses gave you not that bread from heaven, but my Father giveth you the true bread from heaven. For the bread of God is He which cometh down from heaven, and giveth life unto the world"* (vs. 32-33).

What is Jesus' point? Once more, the Lord is exposing their faulty motives. They are only interested in physical food. They have resorted to their original motivation—seeking physical gratification. Jesus explains that He is the only source of satisfaction to those who feel their spiritual hunger and need. He is the true bread of life!

Chapter 11
Objective and Subjective (John 6:34-59)

How does the Lord Jesus proceed to distinguish between the pseudo-followers and the true disciples in this great multitude? He does so by teaching truth.

Truth will ultimately separate between those who say, "This is a hard saying; who can hear it?" (6:60) and those who deem his doctrine to be "the words of eternal life" (6:68).

In specific terms, Jesus teaches both objective truth, i.e. facts concerning the great doctrine of eternal salvation, and subjective truth, i.e. the application of those facts in daily, Christian experience.

It is important in reading John 6 to distinguish between the objective and the subjective and not to confuse the two. Most confusion in this passage among Bible interpreters arises from the failure to rightly divide between what relates to eternal salvation and what concerns Christian experience.

Christ, the Bread of Life (John 6:34-35, 41-42, 48-59)

This passage records the first of the several "I am" statements contained in John's Gospel: "I am the bread of life". These statements clearly identify Jesus of Nazareth with

107

the Jehovah of the Old Testament and are, consequently, another claim to deity.

This sacred name, known among Hebrew scholars as the *tetragrammaton,* speaks of God as self-existent, self-sufficient, self-sustaining, eternally present, and sovereign. The English equivalent "Jehovah" is used over 6800 times in the Old Testament. For Jesus to take that name to himself establishes yet another claim to his essential unity with the Father.

Seven times in John's Gospel, our Lord adds a predicate to the sacred formula to show that he is in himself all that his people will ever need. The first of those predicates is in the chapter before us: "I am the bread of life".

Christ means by this that he satisfies the spiritual appetite of his people: "...he that cometh to me shall never hunger; and he that believeth on me shall never thirst" (v. 35).

Subjective Discipleship

In what sense are these words to be interpreted? The image of "feeding on Jesus Christ" only makes sense if we understand it in terms of daily Christian experience. Though some traditions, like Catholicism, attempt to interpret the imagery here in a ceremonial way, i.e. in terms of receiving "the Eucharist", the language does not suggest something ceremonial. It is instead experiential. Let me explain.

It is understood that only a person with spiritual life possesses a spiritual appetite. The dead sinner does not "hunger and thirst after righteousness" (Mt. 5:4). The "hungry soul" is a soul that has been quickened by Divine grace. Only the "new born babe" has a desire for the "milk of the word" (1 Pet. 2:2).

How does a born-again child of God, then, obtain spiritual nourishment? What satisfies the deepest hunger in his heart? What quenches his spiritual thirst? Christ answers, "I am the bread of life: he that cometh to me [that is, in an experiential sense] shall never hunger; he that believeth on me shall never thirst." As the child of God hears the gospel preached, reads God's word, meditates on the perfections of the Savior, considers the great things that Christ has accomplished, and looks unto Him as the source of his every need, he finds the same kind of inward satisfaction and fulfillment in the Savior that a hungry man might receive from a good meal.

This passage, then, should be interpreted subjectively, or existentially. As we go about our daily lives, we draw strength from Christ. We remember His work on the cross and find peace for a guilty conscience. We consider his perseverance in the face of such great contradiction and find strength to keep going. His name is to our soul what bread is to our bodies. It refreshes and energizes and satisfies the heart like a good meal rejuvenates and gratifies the physical body.

The Jews did not understand how Jesus could fulfill a person's deepest spiritual needs, for they could not get past the fact of his humanity: "Is not this the son of Joseph, whose father and mother we know?" (v. 42). But Jesus was not only fully human. He was also fully divine.

109

Understanding the need to interpret the metaphor experientially is helpful when reading verses 48 and following: "As the living Father hath sent me, and I live by the Father: so he that eateth me, even he shall live by me" (v. 57).

Again, he is not talking about getting "life", but getting a "living". God gives life to all of His people at the point of regeneration. From that day forward, they need daily strength and sustenance to enable them to bear life's burdens, serve their Lord, resist temptation, and fight the good fight of faith. That strength and sustenance comes only from the Lord Jesus Christ, for he is "the living bread."

Objective Salvation (Jno. 6:37-40, 44-47)

Behind every subjective, or experiential, reality is an objective, or doctrinal, fact. If Jesus Christ is bread to some, then what criteria determines those who may receive the benefit? What is the doctrinal basis of daily Christian experience?

The answer is "salvation by grace alone". Only the individual who belongs to Christ by free and sovereign grace has the capacity and the privilege to draw strength and nourishment from Christ. Fellowship with the Savior, in other words, derives from a vital relationship with that Savior, and that relationship is the product of Divine grace. The passage before us details that glorious fact.

Predestination

"All that the Father giveth me..." (v. 37). That the Father gave a people to the Son before the world began is the very foundation of eternal salvation (Jno. 10:29; 17:2, 24; Heb. 2:13). These words express a fundamental Bible truth known as the doctrine of predestination.

The doctrine of predestination teaches that God marked out, with limits, a people as His own, and treasured up grace for them in Christ, that they might be fashioned like His own glorious image in heaven (cf. Rom. 8:29; Eph. 1:4-5, 11). Predestination means that the salvation of sinners begins with God, not with man—that it is His gracious initiative in the covenant before time began, not man's works or decisions in time, that underpins the sinner's hope of bliss (Titus 1:2).

Regeneration

"...shall come to me..." (v. 37). Notice that this is a "certain" salvation: "All...*shall* come". The Lord Jesus did not say they might come, or they can come, or that He hopes they will come. He said they *shall* come.

On what basis can He speak with such certainty? It is sure and certain that all that were given to Him by the Father will come because they will be drawn to Him by irresistible grace. They shall come to Christ in regeneration. That is the sense in which they *shall* come, as verses 44-46 will further establish.

Obviously, every elect does not come to Christ in terms of a gospel profession of faith, for God had an elect people even in

111

Old Testament times, prior to the beginning of the gospel dispensation (Mr. 1:1; Lk. 16:16). How could they profess faith in a gospel that had not been preached yet? Further, God has little ones among the mentally challenged and those who die in infancy. How could such ones "come to Christ" in the sense of gospel profession? And yet the text says "All shall come."

Neither do they all come to Christ in baptism, or in terms of drawing nourishment from Him by means of daily fellowship. The only sense in which "all that the Father" gave to Jesus "shall come" is in terms of regeneration. All that were loved and chosen and marked out by the Father before the foundation of the world will be brought into a vital union and relationship with Jesus Christ because they will be drawn to Him by irresistible grace.

Preservation

"...*and him that cometh to me I will in no wise cast out*" (v. 37b). Not only did God give a people to Christ and draw them to Him in a vital relationship, but He also guarantees their eternal security. They will never, under any circumstances, be "cast out". They will not lose their salvation or be disinherited or disenfranchised.

This glorious truth is reiterated in verse 39: "*And this is the Father's will which hath sent me, that of all which He hath given me I should lose nothing...*". He promises to keep them, to preserve them by His grace, so that none are lost. How glorious is this truth!

112

Redemption

"For I came down from heaven, not to do mine own will, but the will of Him that sent me" (v. 38). The Father's work in predestination and the Spirit's in regeneration are interdependent on the Son's work in redemption. Christ came to execute the Father's Divine purpose (cf. Is. 46:9-11). He came on a mission, with a task before Him.

He did not come to establish a political throne or to improve social and economic standards of living. He came to save His people from their sins (Mt. 1:21), to turn away ungodliness from God's covenant people (Rom. 11:26), to seek and save that which was lost (Lk. 19:10; 1 Tim. 1:15), to give His dear ones life and life more abundant (Jno. 10:10). In a word, He came to do the Father's will (cf. Heb. 10:9-10).

Glorification

"...should lose nothing but raise it up again at the last day" (v. 39). This glorious objective truth of salvation by grace alone culminates with the resurrection of the righteous at the end of time. All that were given to the Son in the covenant, redeemed by the Son at the cross, called by the Holy Spirit in regeneration, and kept safe and secure in His love, will be raised up when Christ returns and glorified, made like unto Him.

From start to finish then, eternal salvation is the work of God, not man. Man's only role is as the happy beneficiary of

113

God's marvelous grace. One evidence that a person is included in the number of those who are thus blessed, as we have seen over and again in John's Gospel, is belief in the Lord Jesus Christ (v. 40). To every believer, the Savior gives assurance that he will not be forgotten, but will be raised up again in the last day.

The Inability of the Natural Man

Our Lord's affirmation in verse 37, "All that the Father giveth me shall come to me" is now explained in verses 44 and 45. Here we learn that Jesus is speaking of that initial "coming to Christ" in regeneration, not the experiential coming to him in gospel faith. Verse 44 explains why their "coming" is such a certainty, i.e. because they are "drawn" by God.

"No man can come to me..." (v. 44). The helping verb "can" denotes ability. Previously we learned that the natural man does not have the desire to come to Christ (5:40). Here, we learn that his plight is even more hopeless. Not only does he lack the desire, the natural man also lacks the capacity to come to Christ.

Such are the depths of human depravity. The sinner would not come to Christ if he could, and he could not come if he would (cf. 1 Cor. 2:14). He is dead in trespasses and in sins—utterly incapacitated to spiritual things and unresponsive to stimuli (cf. Eph. 2:1; Rom. 5:12; Jno. 3:3,5). His natural condition is so averse to spiritual things that every motion is

114

away from God (Is. 53:6; 1 Pet. 2:25). By nature man says unto God, "Depart from me, for I desire not the knowledge of thy ways" (Job 21:14). He does not seek God, love God, or fear God (Rom. 3:10-18).

The scope of this tragic condition is universal: *"No man* can come...". Neither the wealthy businessman or the homeless beggar; neither the famous celebrity nor the infamous villain; neither the nobility nor the commoner; neither the intellectual nor the ignoramus – no man can. Left in this fallen condition, the sinner will never move Godward. He can't. He hasn't the ability to take the first step. He is dead in sin.

The Blessed Exception

"No man can come to me except..." (v. 44). John Bunyan once called the word "except" in verse 44 "the blessed exception". Thank God there is an exception, else no one would ever be saved.

What is the exception? Already we have established that it has nothing to do with man's social or economic status. Jesus does not suggest that "no man can come except the extremely attractive, or the especially talented, or the incredibly astute individual". No. The exception originates not in man's nature but in God's grace. Grace alone makes the exception to the exceeding sinfulness of sin.

Irresistible Grace

"...except the Father which hath sent me draw him..." (v. 44). The use of the verb "to draw" asserts the immediacy (i.e. without the use of means or media), irresistibility, and the efficacy of this work.

The word suggests the image of someone drawing water from a well. Just as one does not entice water to get into the bucket, so God does not woo sinners to salvation. Instead, He reaches down and by an act of His own sovereign power, acts upon the sinner and brings him into a vital union with Jesus Christ.

Every time this word is used in the New Testament, it always means to compel by force—literally, to drag. Never does it mean to invite, entice, or woo (cf. Acts 16:19; 21:30; Jas. 2:6; Jno. 12:32; 21:6,11; 18:10).

Taught of God

At the point of regeneration, God writes His law upon the heart: *"And they shall be all taught of God. Every man therefore that hath heard, and hath learned of the Father, cometh unto me"* (v. 45).

Note that the education under consideration is not "about the Father", but "of the Father"—that is, God is the source or the origin of this teaching. When He writes His law in the heart (cf. Rom. 2:14-15; Heb. 8:11), He imparts both the desire and the ability to function in the spiritual realm (Phi. 2:13). Thus "drawn to Christ" in a new and living relationship, the child of grace possesses an inner principle, or "law of the inward man" (Rom. 7:22), that influences and affects his ethical conduct (Rom. 2:14; 1 Jno. 2:29). He doesn't need instruction to "love his neighbor", for he has been "taught of God to love one another" (1 Ths. 4:9) so that it is a divine instinct within his heart. This "inner witness" (1 Jno. 5:10) gives him the ability now to receive the external witness of the true gospel, so that belief in the Lord Jesus Christ and a reciprocal response to the gospel message is an evidence that one has been drawn to Christ (v. 47).

It was our Lord's "sovereign grace" sermon, then, that separated the spurious from the true followers. He began chapter 6 with a great multitude following him. He concludes the chapter with the few disciples that had been with him from early on. Those simply caught up in this new "movement" or "fad" were whittled away by his unambiguous proclamation of human inability, sovereign election, and effectual calling.

In a cultural climate of political-correctness and religious climate of denominational competition for numbers and noses (e. g. the "mega-church movement"), more and more professing Christians have opted to soft-peddle the more offensive and embarrassing aspects of Christian doctrine in favor of a more generic, feel-good, message.

It is a perilous thing when Christian people crave popularity and fame. Inevitably they opt to compromise truth for the sake of numerical increase. Such compromise often comes in the form of adding unbiblical "programs" and other worldly innovations to church-life, justifying it in terms of an opportunity to increase conversions.

At other times, it comes in the form of soft-peddling the gospel message. The doctrine of total depravity is dismissed in favor of a less-offensive emphasis on inherent self-worth. The doctrine of election is jettisoned for an emphasis on man's free-will. Particular redemption is replaced with general atonement and a universal offer of salvation if the sinner will just accept it. Immediate regeneration is discarded in favor of decisional regeneration. All of this is done to make the "hard doctrine" of salvation by grace alone a bit more palatable to modern tastes.

Jesus knew that it was preferable to have a few, loyal disciples who genuinely believed than to have a multitude of self-centered, fickle, "what's-in-it-for-me" followers. Would that many Christians would learn that lesson today and restore truth to its rightful place of preeminence above popularity and programs!

Chapter 12
Jesus at the Feast of Tabernacles (John 7)

A *fter these things Jesus walked in Galilee: for he would not walk in Jewry, because the Jews sought to kill him"* (7:1). This verse signals a transition in the personal ministry of the Lord Jesus as John develops it in his Gospel. Prior to this point, Jesus has alternated venues between Jerusalem and Galilee. The mass exodus of his Galilean followers in chapter six, however, marks the end of his Galilean ministry. The balance of his ministry, henceforth, will take place in Jerusalem.

For a bit longer, however, Jesus continued to walk among the common people of Galilee (albeit not among the religious leaders, i.e. *"Jewry"*), showing his reticence to leave them. The fact that he did not presumptuously expose himself to the religious leaders teaches us *"not to court danger [or]...unnecessarily expose ourselves before our enemies...So it is our duty to endeavor by all wise means and precautions to protect and preserve ourselves, that we may have opportunities for further service."*[1]

"Now the Jews' feast of tabernacles was at hand" (7:2). Approximately six months have elapsed since the Feast of

---

[1] A. W. Pink, *Gospel of John*, p. 370. Compare Jno. 11:53-54.

Passover, referenced in John 6:4, and the Feast of Tabernacles, referenced here in John 7:2 (cf. Lev. 23:5 and Lev. 23:34). The Feast of Tabernacles was the longest festival of the Jewish year (lasting seven days) and was followed by the Jewish New Year and the Day of Atonement, or *Yom Kippur*. It was a time to celebrate God's providence for the children of Israel in the wilderness and to remember the pilgrim nature of their existence.

The Jews would typically make a pilgrimage to Jerusalem (cf. Deut. 16:16) and live in booths for seven days. The highlights of the week were a ceremonial water-drawing to commemorate how God had provided them water in the wilderness (Num. 20:2-13) and a ceremonial lamp-lighting. The first provides the setting for our Lord's actions in 7:37-39 and the second for his words in 8:12.

The background for the Feast of Tabernacles is recorded in Leviticus 23:34-36, 39-44. Numbers 29:12-40 gives instructions for the sacrifices and offerings that were required at this feast. Exodus 23:16, however, mentions a further fact. The Feast of Tabernacles was also the time of in-gathering, or what we would typically call a "harvest festival." For seven days, the people not only commemorated their pilgrim experience, but celebrated God's abundant provision in caring for their temporal needs. It was, therefore, the most joyful feast of the year.

The physical brothers of Jesus (who likely still lived in Nazareth of Galilee) urged him to go to Jerusalem for the purpose of exposing himself as the Messiah at the Feast (vs. 3-4). That their motives were less than genuine is evident from verse 5: *"For neither did his brethren believe in him."* Their words amount to a carnal challenge, saying, "If you're such a hot shot, prove it in the big city." Some of his own brothers would later be numbered among his followers (Acts 1:14), but at this point, each disbelieved. The prejudice of personal familiarity is frequently a significant obstacle to faith.[2]

Our Lord's response indicates just how completely his life was governed by the Father's will and his sense of the Divine timing of his redemptive purpose: *"My time is not yet come: but your time is always ready. The world cannot hate you; but me it hateth, because I testify of it, that the works thereof are evil. Go ye up unto this feast: I go not up yet unto this feast; for my time is not yet full come"* (vs. 6-8). His words anticipate a time when he would reveal himself publicly, albeit not in Messianic conquest and glory but, rather, in Messianic suffering and humiliation.

"When he had said these words unto them, he abode still in Galilee. But when his brethren were gone up, then went he also up unto the feast, not openly, but as it were in secret" (vs. 9-10). With the tension mounting, the Lord Jesus refused to travel to Jerusalem in caravan with his brothers. Instead, he waited until they left, then made the journey himself, alone.

---

[2] For example, consider the familiar case of prodigal children among those in pastoral ministry today. Although there may be various reasons for this phenomenon, personal familiarity is certainly a contributing factor in some cases.

It is important to note that Jesus was careful to obey the Law in every respect. Deuteronomy 16:16 required every Jewish male to present himself in Jerusalem at this Feast, and our Lord was submissive to God's Law to fulfill it in every detail.

It is also important to note that He did it in a way that would avoid publicity. He knew that the tension surrounding Him was increasing and that the animosity of the religious leaders, i.e. "*Jewry*" (v. 1), coupled with public curiosity about Him could easily make for a chaotic scene at the feast.

Hence, when the caravan consisting of his brothers arrived without him, the people wondered where he was and debated among themselves about his identity (vs. 11-14). Meanwhile, he arrived in Jerusalem without public incident and mingled undetected among the people for a couple of days.

"Now about the midst of the feast Jesus went up into the temple, and taught. And the Jews marveled, saying, How knoweth this man letters, having never learned?" (vs. 14-15). Having escaped the distraction and confusion that a public entrance into Jerusalem would have engendered (for his time was not yet come – v. 6), Jesus was able to make his appearance in way that would have the greatest impact, i.e. in the context of teaching God's word.

It has been said that a good boxer never fights in the back alleys, but saves his boxing for the ring. The same is true for our Lord. He carefully avoided celebrity status, but maximized the impact of this opportunity to teach and preach God's word.

Though the Holy Spirit does not reveal the content of His teaching on this occasion, He does reveal its effect. The people *"marveled saying, How knoweth this man letters, having never learned?"* Unlike the scribes, Jesus had not been schooled in the rabbinical seminaries and classrooms. Yet he taught God's word with greater substance, clarity and power than the people had ever heard.

The Lord answered their questions as follows: *"My doctrine is not mine, but His that sent me. If any man will do His will, he shall know of the doctrine, whether it be of God, or whether I speak of myself. He that speaketh of himself seeketh his own glory: but he that seeketh His glory that sent him, the same is true, and no unrighteousness is in him"* (vs. 16-18). In these words, Jesus lays to rest any question about his motives. Unlike the religious leaders of his day, Jesus was not driven by personal ambition. He was not pursuing His own agenda or trying to further His own career. In fulfillment of the prophecy in Isaiah 42:2, he did not *"cry nor lift up nor cause his voice to be heard in the street"* in a quest for personal fame.

In this matter, Jesus distinguishes himself from the religious leaders. They were characteristically motivated by self-interest, turning the service of God into a professional career opportunity. Instead, Jesus Christ was zealous for His Father's glory. Everything He did was for the honor of God, not for Himself. What a powerful lesson this is to everyone who seeks to serve in the Church of our Lord and Savior Jesus Christ!

Confusion about Jesus (7:25-39)

The confusion surrounding Jesus in Jerusalem during the Feast of Tabernacles is John's focus in John 7:25-53. It is common for people to make hasty and faulty judgments, i.e. to judge according to the appearance, instead of judging righteously (7:24). These verses highlight that human tendency and reveal the unreliability of public opinion.

Confusion Among the Common People

"Then said some of them of Jerusalem, Is not this he, whom they seek to kill? But, lo, he speaketh boldly, and they say nothing unto him. Do the rulers know indeed that this is the Christ? Howbeit we know this man whence he is: but when Christ cometh, no man knoweth whence he is" (vs. 24-27). If it were not so sad, these verses would be somewhat comical. The common people of Jerusalem are confused whether or not Jesus is the "wanted" man about whom they've heard. If the rulers want him dead, they wonder, why do they permit him to speak unchallenged? Then the question begins to circulate, *"Do the rulers know indeed that this is the Christ?"* How sad it is when people cease to think for themselves and allow their leaders to think for them! "What do the rulers think about this man? Are they sure that he is the Messiah, or not?"

We might paraphrase Jesus' answer to the whispering crowd in verses 28-29 as follows: "Yes, you do indeed know me and my hometown; nevertheless, what you do not realize is that my real home of origin is heaven. I have come to do the Father's will."

Some of the people then attempted unsuccessfully to apprehend him, but *"his hour was not yet come"* (v. 30). This verse reveals that man had no power over the Lord Jesus Christ. When it was time for him to go to the cross, he would do so voluntarily. His life would not be taken from him. He would lay it down of his own accord (cf. 10:18).

Others *"believed on him,"* but were yet unclear about his true identity: *"And many of the people believed on him, and said, When Christ cometh, will he do more miracles than these which this man hath done?"* (v. 31). Though it is evident that these folks were not mature "believers," yet the implication is that they felt an inner inclination or leaning toward him, though their minds were unclear about his identity.

Confusion Among the Officers

When the religious leaders learned that the common people whispered these things about Jesus, they determined that it was time to put a stop to the chaos. They sent officers to apprehend him (v. 32). When the officers arrived, however, Jesus said unto them, *"Yet a little while am I with you, and then I go unto him that sent me. Ye shall seek me, and shall not find me: and where I am, thither ye cannot come"* (vs. 33-34).

It would be approximately six months before the crucifixion.[3] Jesus' words, then, mean "It is not yet time to apprehend me, but it won't be much longer." Obviously, Jesus is working according to the Father's schedule, not man's timing. He, not the religious leaders among the Jews, is in charge of the situation. The words *"you shall seek me and shall not find me"* anticipate his resurrection.

Such an unexpected pronouncement had the effect of stunning the officers. They questioned each other, *"Whither will he go, that we shall not find him? Will he go unto the dispersed among the Gentiles, and teach the Gentiles? What manner of saying is this that he said, Ye shall seek me, and shall not find me: and where I am, thither ye cannot come?"* (vs. 35-36). They could not decipher the meaning of His words. Of course, Christ spoke of His return to heaven. But such an idea never even occurred to them. It takes illumination from the Holy Spirit to be able to perceive the meaning and significance of the things of God.

Never Man Spake as This Man (7:40-53)

The public confusion concerning Jesus' identity continued even to the last day of the Feast of Tabernacles: *"Many of the people therefore, when they heard this saying, said, Of a truth this is the Prophet. Others said, This is the Christ. But some said, Shall Christ come out of Galilee? Hath not the Scripture said, That Christ cometh of the seed of David, and out of the town of Bethlehem,*

---

[3] The Feast of the Tabernacles occurred near the end of September, according to our Western calendar; Christ would be crucified during the next Feast of Passover in early April.

where David was? So there was a division among the people because of him. And some of them would have taken him; but no man laid hands on him" (7:40-44).

Again, we see here an object lesson concerning the unreliability of public opinion. Some associated Jesus with the Mosaic prophecy in Deuteronomy 18:15: *"The Lord thy God will raise up unto thee a Prophet from the midst of thee, of thy brethren, like unto me; unto him ye shall hearken."* It seems, however, that they did not connect that "Prophet" with the Messiah. Others, identified him as the Messiah, saying, *"This is the Christ"* but some questioned, *"Shall Christ come out of Galilee?"* The very Messiah stood among them, but they knew him not (cf. 1:11). *"So there was a division among the people because of him"* (v. 43). It has ever been so that the true Christ has been a divisive influence in this world, separating between true believers and unbelievers (cf. Lk. 12:51-52).

When the officers who were sent to apprehend Jesus reported back to the religious leaders who had sent them, they explained their failure to fulfill their mission by saying, *"Never man spake like this man"* (vs. 45-46). They had been sent to physically arrest him; instead, he had arrested them by his words. The unique content and power of his teaching had stopped their mad campaign to apprehend him. They completely forgot their mission and goal in the wake of his words. Never had they felt so awkward and "out of their league" as they did in the presence of Christ.

Never man spake like this man. A truer testimony has never been given. All of man's important decisions pale into insignificance in the light of Christ's truth. These religious leaders and officials had contrived a plan to silence Jesus, but the sheer power of His teaching caused the pawns sent to carry out the plan to forego (and perhaps forget) their intended purpose.

What a sublime sentence for meditation! *Never a man spake like this man*—in terms of His power to create spiritual life in the hearts of His people by the sovereign command of His spoken voice (Jno. 5:25; 1 Pet. 1:23; Heb. 4:12-13); in terms of the preciousness of His promises (Mt. 5:3ff; 11:28; Jno. 14:1-3; Mt. 28:20); in terms of the tone of authority and certainty He assumed (Mt. 7:28-29); in terms of the way he communicated in language common folk would understand (Mt. 13:3); in terms of the applicability of his teaching to the situation at hand (Lk. 7:40-48); in terms of his ability to confound those who sought to entrap him (Mt. 22:46).

The religious leaders responded, *"Are ye also deceived? Have any of the rulers or of the Pharisees believed on him? But this people who knoweth not the law are cursed"* (7:47-49). How quickly do the proud sinner's true colors shine through! The sneering snobbery of these religious leaders is evident in the contemptuous way they refer to the common folk, i.e. *"this people who know not the law."* They might as well have called them "riff-raff" or "rabble." What these men who fancied themselves to be important failed to realize is that *"not many wise men, not many mighty, not many noble are called"* (1 Cor. 1:26-28). It is not until a man humbles himself and admits his own unworthiness that he is ready to receive the gospel of Christ.

The conspiracy to apprehend Jesus is further stalled by Nicodemus, who warns them about the danger of proceeding before they have evidence (vs. 50-51). The leaders then turn their ire on him (v. 52). It is evident that they will not rest until Jesus is exterminated.

Chapter 13
Jesus' Conflict with the Pharisees (John 8)

I n the wake of the failed arrest attempt while Jesus attended the Feast of Tabernacles, the Jewish rulers ramped up the pressure, attempting to entrap Jesus and publicly challenging his doctrine. John 8 records this note of increasing tension and shows the wisdom of the Lord Jesus Christ in countering the insidious attempts to find occasion to accuse him.

The Adulterous Woman (8:1-11)

Biblical critics dismiss the first eleven verses of chapter 8 because, they say, the passage is not in the better manuscripts. The simple answer to this criticism is that the *"them"* of verse 12 has no context or reference point if verses 2-11 are omitted. Since the previous day concluded with the disciples returning to their own homes (cf. 7:53) and Jesus retreating to the Mount of Olives (cf. 8:1), then what is the context for the clause that begins verse 12: *"Then Jesus spake again unto them..."*? Who is the *"them"* if verses 2-11 are not authentic. The details of verse 2, however, that introduce the narrative of the woman caught in adultery—*"And early in the morning [Jesus] came again into the temple, and all the people came unto him; and he sat down, and taught them"* —give context to statement that Jesus resumed his teaching to the temple congregation in verse 12. Apart from a technical debate, then, the context itself indicates that this passage must be authentic.

The more elaborate answer is that these "better manuscripts" refer to the Latin Vulgate manuscripts such as the *Codex Sinaiticus* and *Codex Vaticanus,* the manuscript family employed by Westcott and Hort in the production of many modern Bible versions. Whether the Latin Vulgate family is "better" is arguable. The Authorized Version of the Bible was translated from the *Textus Receptus,* or Received Text (also called "the Majority Text" due to the preponderance of supporting fragments and codices that are extant) deriving from the Byzantine family of manuscript evidence, the authenticity and accuracy of which may be demonstrated with compelling arguments.

Conventional wisdom indicates that the real motive behind an attempt to discredit this passage is antagonism to the message of grace. This passage records the familiar story of Christ forgiving the adulterous woman. Is it possible that the Lord Jesus displays too much grace toward this woman to suit some people? Did the officials and priests behind the Latin Vulgate manuscripts omit this passage because they feared it would encourage people to commit adultery?

Entrapment

Note, first, the effort made by the scribes and Pharisees to entrap the Lord Jesus Christ. As Jesus teaches the people in the temple, the scribes and Pharisees *"brought unto him a woman taken in adultery"* and said, *"Master, this woman was taken in adultery, in the very act. Now Moses in the law commanded us, that such should be stoned: but what sayest thou? This they said, tempting him, that they might have to accuse him"* (vs. 3-6).

The plot to apprehend him on the previous day had failed. So now, the religious leaders hatch a new scheme. It is their design to set him up, to tempt him to contradict Moses, to stump him with a theological problem, to trap him in hypocrisy. Arthur Pink comments on this new conspiracy, "The roar of the 'lion' had failed; now we are to behold the wiles of the 'serpent'."[1]

The dilemma Jesus faced was simply this: If he said "Release her," they could accuse him before the Sanhedrin of violating the law of God and discredit him before the people as a heretic. If he said, "Stone her," they could accuse him of sedition before the Roman government, for vassal nations under Roman occupation had no authority to prosecute capital cases. The Scribes and Pharisees appeared to have Jesus impaled on the horns of a dilemma.

It is important here to note that these religious leaders were not alarmed at her conduct. They were interested only to use

---

[1] A. W. Pink, *Exposition of the Gospel of John*, p. 419.

her to discredit Jesus before the people. The Pharisees' exploitation of this woman differs little from her lover's exploitation of her (who must have been caught with her but is suspiciously absent on this occasion).

Conviction

How would Jesus respond to this public challenge? Interestingly, *"Jesus stooped down, and with his finger wrote on the ground, as though he heard them not"* (v. 6b). We are not told what he wrote. Was he merely doodling in the sand? I personally doubt it, for wasting time, stalling for an answer, and engaging in trivialities seems completely foreign to the character sketch of the Lord Jesus painted in the four Gospels. That he wrote something of significance and relevance to this particular set of circumstances is evident, as the subsequent passage makes clear.

The act of crouching to write on the ground is a kind of "back to school" posture such as a teacher would assume in communicating the most elementary lessons to little children. As such, Jesus' puzzling behavior may very well be an object lesson to these religious leaders that they have overlooked the most basic of principles, namely that people are a greater priority than rules and regulations (cf. Mt. 9:13).

Mistaking his silence for embarrassment, the Pharisees *"continued asking him"* (v. 7). Then he stood up and said, *"He that is without sin among you, let him first cast a stone at her"* (v. 7b).

Is this verse a prohibition against passing judgment in every case? Does verse 7 preclude the exercise of church discipline? Does it negate all judgment? No doubt, it is often cited to stress that very point. If that is the intention of the text, however, no decision regarding what constitutes righteous and what constitutes wicked conduct would ever be appropriate. I suggest that our Lord does not here prohibit the legitimate practice of judging whether conduct is ethical or not.

What, then, is Jesus' point? His point is simply that this situation is not quite what it appears to be. Where is the man caught with her? The law required both to be stoned. Perhaps he was one of their own, protected now from public scandal by his "brethren." Secondly, their motives are clearly less than honorable. They have publicly interrupted Jesus while teaching the people and challenged him to solve this riddle between justice and mercy.

Jesus then stooped down a second time and wrote again in the dirt. Could it be that he wrote the name of the absent party? Is it possible that he began to write specific sins that this woman's accusers had committed in their own lives? Whatever he wrote, it was sufficient to *convict them in their own consciences*" (vs. 8-9), so that they departed from the gathering with slumped shoulders. They had come to accuse Him. They leave with embarrassment that they are the ones who have been accused.

Grace

When the religious leaders were gone, Jesus asked the woman, *"Where are those thine accusers? Hath no man condemned thee?"* (v. 10). This blessed sentence expresses the very heart and soul of the message of grace. This is the question the gospel posits to the little child of grace: "Where are your accusers? Can anyone condemn you?" The gospel proclaims that because of the substitutionary sacrifice of the Lord Jesus Christ in the stead of God's elect, no one can lay any charge against them—none can condemn (cf. Rom. 8:33-34).

She replied *"No man, Lord."* Then he said, *"Neither do I condemn thee: go, and sin no more"* (v. 11). What amazing and marvelous grace does our Lord here extend to this sinful woman! It is, indeed, too much grace for the proud, self-righteous Pharisees. But to those who know themselves to be vile sinners, it is welcome news. Indeed, it is the only message that will suit their case.

Did she get away with sin? No. She had suffered embarrassment already before the people. Further, Christ would bear that sin in her stead and atone for it on the cross. Also, who knows how God might have chastened her for it in her own life? Indeed, justice was not sacrificed on this occasion, but grace and mercy was gloriously extended to this woman.

Was Christ easy on sin? No, again. He charged her, *"Go and sin no more."* The forgiveness of sins in the life of a penitent child of God is often the greatest incentive to live a life of holiness from that point forward. Far from being a license to ungodliness, grace is an incentive to godliness (cf. Titus 2:11-12), forgiveness promotes godly fear (Ps. 130:4; 2 Cor. 7:11), and the goodness of God leads to repentance (Rom. 2:4). May it prove to be so in our lives also.

How might this forgiven and penitent woman comply with Jesus' exhortation to stop sinning? Verse 12 answers, by following Jesus Christ, the Light of the world: *"Then spake Jesus again unto them, saying, I am the light of the world: he that followeth me shall not walk in darkness, but shall have the light of life."* The metaphor of darkness speaks of sin and ungodliness. If the forgiven sinner wants to break with old, sinful habits, the secret to success is to stay very close to Jesus Christ, for following Jesus is the way to avoid stumbling along in the darkness of sin and rebellion.

The Public Challenge (8:13-59)

The Pharisees' antagonism to Jesus has reached a boiling-point in John 8. No longer content to try to trick or entrap him, they publicly challenge him in debate on the legal validity of his testimony.

Animosity Rooted in Prejudice (vs. 13-18)

"The Pharisees therefore said unto him, Thou bearest record of thyself; thy record is not true" (v. 13). They claimed that his testimony was not legally valid because it lacked

corroboration. Deuteronomy 17:6 and 19:15 required that testimony in every court proceeding must be confirmed by two or three witnesses before it could be considered valid. The Pharisees argue that Jesus is simply "blowing his own horn" and that he lacks the necessary supporting witnesses.

Jesus answers the charge by appealing once more to his heavenly origin as the reason his claim was credible: *"Though I bear record of myself, yet my record is true: for I know whence I came, and whither I go; but ye cannot tell whence I come, and whither I go"* (v. 14). His argument is clear. When an ambassador arrives at a foreign court, he alone knows the purpose of his mission and the message he is sent to convey. The sole business of the court to which he is sent is to validate his credentials. Once those credentials are verified, they have no reason to question the message that he brings or demand that it be corroborated by multiple messengers.

Jesus claims that he has been sent from heaven and has the credentials to prove it; consequently, his message is credible: *"Ye judge after the flesh; I judge no man. And yet if I judge, my judgment is true: for I am not alone, but I and the Father that sent me. It is also written in your law, that the testimony of two men is true. I am one that bear witness of myself, and the Father that sent me beareth witness of me"* (vs. 15-18). What credentials does he site as evidence that he has a heavenly origin? The reference to the Father bearing witness of him speaks of the miracles and signs he had performed. Already in John's Gospel, the Holy Spirit has recorded five of the seven signs. These are certainly sufficient evidence to make his message, even though it is a message of self-testimony, credible.

Jesus' point is simply that the Pharisees were applying a legal precedent to a moral issue. It would be comparable to rejecting a public speaker's right to advance an idea in public on the grounds that an attorney must have a license to practice law. The burden of proof concerning the credibility of the public speaker rests on his audience and their capacity to make a judgment of plausibility, not on legal precedent. Albert Barnes comments, "In a *legal* or *criminal* case such testimony would not be admitted, yet in an argument on *moral* subjects, about the will and purpose of him who sent him, it would not be right to reject the testimony of one who gave so many proofs that he came from God."[2]

Unbelief Rooted in Depravity (vs. 19-24)

If the evidences that Jesus had a Divine and heavenly origin were so plentiful, then why did the Pharisees refuse to believe? Jesus answers by showing the connection between unbelief and the native depravity that is in the human heart.

"Then said they unto him, Where is thy Father? Jesus answered, Ye neither know me, nor my Father: if ye had known me, ye should have known my Father also" (v. 19). The Pharisees' prejudicial blindness to Jesus' identity was not due to a lack of education, but to their own unregenerate hearts. This native depravity is

---

[2] *Barnes' Notes on the New Testament*, p. 305. [emphasis original]

the source of all antagonism to the Lord Jesus Christ in the world.

"Then said Jesus again unto them, I go my way, and ye shall seek me, and shall die in your sins: whither I go, ye cannot come...Ye are from beneath; I am from above: ye are of this world; I am not of this world. I said therefore unto you, that ye shall die in your sins: for if ye believe not that I am he, ye shall die in your sins" (vs. 21, 23-24). In this passage, our Lord predicts his departure. Then he adds, *"whither I go, ye cannot come."* Later in John's Gospel, he will tell his disciples, *"whither I go, ye cannot follow me **now**, but ye shall follow me hereafter"* (cf. 13:36). To these wicked men, however, he simply states the impossibility of their salvation without any future prospect of a remedy– *"...ye cannot come."*

This kind of unbelief that refuses to acknowledge the evidence while continuing its mad campaign of antagonism against the Lord originates in the unregenerate heart. Unless grace intervenes to radically change such an individual, he/she will die in his sins.

Jesus' Defense (vs. 25-29)

The patience Jesus exercised with these obstinate opponents is truly amazing. *"Then said they unto him, Who art thou? And Jesus said unto them, Even the same that I said unto you from the beginning"* (v. 25). He had claimed to be the Light of the world, the Bread that came down from heaven, and the fount of living water. From any of these they might have grasped his Messianic identity, except for their prejudicial blindness.

Jesus might have condemned them further, but judgment and condemnation was not the purpose of his first advent (v. 26; cf. 3:17-19). Their obstinate unbelief, opposition to and animosity toward the Lord Jesus Christ is evidence of their depravity and forecasts their final condemnation unless grace intervenes. But the time of sentencing was not yet. Final judgment and condemnation would attend Christ's second coming, not his first.

In verse 28, Jesus points to his crucifixion as the event that will prove beyond doubt that he is the Messiah and that the Father endorsed his doctrine: *"When ye have lifted up the Son of man, then shall ye know that I am he, and that I do nothing of myself; but as my Father hath taught me, I speak these things."* The evidence to which he refers is the crucifixion miracles, the earthquakes and darkness that attended his death, and his subsequent resurrection.

Then Jesus takes comfort in the fact that heaven was on his side even though he met with such vicious opposition on earth: *"And he that sent me is with me: the Father hath not left me alone; for I do always those things that please him"* (v. 29). Albert Barnes writes, "It is a small matter to have men opposed to us, if we have a conscience void of offence, and evidence that we please God...Enoch, before his translation had this testimony, that he pleased God."[3]

---

[3] *Barnes Notes on the New Testament*, p. 307.

Believers, But Not Disciples (vs. 30-32)

There is an interesting sidebar in verses 30-32 to this tense conversation with the Pharisees. *"As he spake these words, many believed on him. Then said Jesus to those Jews which believed on him, If ye continue in my word, then are ye my disciples indeed; and ye shall know the truth, and the truth shall make you free."*

We can be happy that the Holy Spirit has been pleased to reveal to us such a blessed exception to this adversarial scene. It teaches us that the entire crowd was not unregenerate—the whole mob was not wicked. In fact, a significant number of them, i.e. *"many,"* were born again children of God.

That's not simply my opinion. The Holy Spirit says so: *"Many believed on him."* Barnes says, "While there were many that became more obstinate and hardened under [Jesus teaching], there were many also who by the same truth were made penitent and believing.[4]

A number of commentators suggest that this was a spurious faith—that it was not genuine. But I would ask, "On what *textual* basis may we make such a claim?" The text clearly says they *"believed on Jesus,"* not that they had a moment of sympathetic consensus, or that they briefly allowed their minds to contemplate the thought that he might be the Messiah. Biblical inspiration says they *"believed."*

Of course, the Scriptures teach that *"whosoever believeth on Him hath everlasting life"* (3:36; 6:47); that *"whosoever believeth that Jesus is the Christ is born of God"* (1 Jno. 5:1); that

---

[4] Ibid. p. 307.

"whosoever heareth my words and believeth on Him that sent me hath everlasting life, and shall not come into condemnation but is passed from death unto life" (5:24). These people were children of God.

Other Bible students dismiss their faith in Christ as illegitimate because it does not translate into good works. But doesn't the passage also indicate that much? They believed, but they were not yet disciples, or followers of the Lord Jesus Christ (v. 31). Detractors of my position would argue that this cannot refer to genuine faith, for genuine faith is only evidenced by good works (cf. Jas. 2:20ff).

How should we answer? We should answer by saying, "Indeed, genuine faith is only proved by good works, so far as the judgment of *other people* is concerned." We cannot see into someone's heart, and thus the only way we can see faith is by by means of godly actions, or good works. The Holy Spirit, however, can see into the heart and identify true, as opposed to spurious, faith. And what he saw on this occasion was that these people believed.

This passage teaches us that all believers are not necessarily disciples—that a person may believe in the heart but fall short of confessing with the mouth and following with the feet. If a person wants true freedom, however, he must follow the Lord Jesus in discipleship, and the truth will make him free.

Freedom & Bondage (vs. 32-36)

"And ye shall know the truth, and the truth shall make you free" (v. 32). This important sentence from the lips of the Savior is frequently cited as a basic axiom or principle for ethical conduct. A parent might coerce a child to honesty, for instance, by reminding him, "The truth will make you free." There is more here, however, than a simple moral platitude. By "the truth" Jesus means "the truth as it is in Christ Jesus" (cf. Eph. 4:21) as verse 36 makes clear: *"If the Son therefore shall make you free, ye shall be free indeed."*

"The truth" that is under consideration here, in other words, refers to the Christian gospel (cf. Col. 1:5-6; Gal. 2:5; 3:1). That the truth of God's grace in Christ can liberate the believer from the bondage of legalism, the slavery of self-righteousness and pride, and the oppression of inward passion and corrupt attitudes, is a glorious fact. The Pharisees were at that moment in bondage to the law. Jesus announces that in the path of Christian discipleship, they would find emancipation from that bondage.

The premise of Jesus' claim is that sin brings bondage. Apart from Christ and a knowledge of His truth, people are captives and slaves to sin, obeying the dictates of the carnal nature (see Rom. 6:16-17, 19-20; Gal. 4:3, 9). The gospel of Christ has the power to break those shackles and set the prisoner free. The religion of Jesus Christ, in other words, is not merely another form of bondage by which certain men

144

exercise control over other men. It alone is true freedom, and everyone outside of its influence is in bondage (Mt. 11:28-30).

"They answered him, We be Abraham's seed and were never in bondage to any man; how sayest thou, Ye shall be made free?" (v. 33). The Pharisees thought Jesus was speaking in terms of political slavery. They claimed to be the descendants of Abraham through Isaac, who was born of the free woman, not through Ishmael, who was born of the bond-woman. "We are the true Israelites and have never been anyone's slave," they claimed. But what a silly thing to say seeing that their fathers had been slaves in Egypt, in Babylon, to the Assyrians, and were at that moment under a very grievous bondage to the Romans! It is evident that, at this very moment, these Pharisees were under a bondage of deception, unwilling to acknowledge their own faults, as well as a bondage of passion and irritation that compelled them to oppose the words of Jesus.

"Whosoever committeth sin is the servant of sin. And the servant abideth not in the house for ever: but the Son abideth for ever. If the Son therefore shall make you free, ye shall be free indeed" (vs. 34-36). Here our Lord corrects them. He explains that he had not been referring to political bondage at all, but to a spiritual slavery, a bondage to sinful passions and attitudes. His point is that a person is a slave to sin to the extent that sin rules in his life. And further, a slave is not entitled to ongoing privileges in the family. "At any point," he tells the Pharisees, "you may be rejected from the blessings of God because of

your disobedience and rebellion. But if you are made free by the Son, you may continue to enjoy the favors of the house of God."

The gospel of the Lord Jesus Christ can indeed make a man free from life dominating sins and the influence of sinful passions. It can make him calm and peaceful, meek and humble, loving and happy in the Lord. This is the kind of freedom enjoyed by true disciples of the Lord Jesus Christ.

A Portrait of the Unregenerate Sinner (vs. 37-50)

John 8:37-50 provides one of the most detailed, personal portraits of a sinner, apart from grace, in the Bible. If Romans 3:10-18 is a verbal and theoretical description of man by nature, John 8:37-50 is a visual and practical description.

These Pharisees thought that they were God's spiritual children because they were Abraham's natural descendants. But Paul makes it clear that just because someone is of the seed of Abraham, i.e. a physical Jew, that does not mean that he is also a child of God (cf. Rom. 9:7-8). In fact, salvation is by grace, not race.

Until a person is regenerated by the direct and immediate work of the Holy Spirit in the heart, he is does not have a vital relationship with God: *"For he is not a Jew which is one outwardly; neither is that circumcision which is outward in the flesh: but he is a Jew which is one inwardly; and circumcision is that of the heart, in the spirit, and not in the letter; whose praise is not of men, but of God"* (Rom. 2:28-29).

146

Consider the various features of this unflattering portrait. The first characteristic of the unregenerate man is **animosity**: "*I know that ye are Abraham's seed; but ye seek to kill me, because my word hath no place in you*" (vs. 37-38). These Pharisees were not merely passively indifferent to Christ and his teaching; they were actively antagonistic. Their opposition to the truth was so intense that they were willing to act upon it. They wanted to kill Jesus.

There is a difference between someone who simply wants to "let well enough alone," to "live and let live," and to disagree peaceably, and someone whose animosity is so intense that they want to put a detractor to death. Paul describes the hostility toward God that resides in the heart of natural man in Romans 8:7: "*The carnal mind is enmity against God; it is not subject to the law of God, neither indeed can be.*" The word "enmity" means *animus, antagonism, hostility.*

Like these Pharisees, Saul of Tarsus sought to act on his antagonism toward Christ by pursuing a ruthless campaign of persecution against the church (cf. Phi. 3:6; Acts 9:1-2; 26:9-11). In 1 Timothy 1:13, he describes his pre-Damascus Road life in terms of *blasphemy, persecution,* and *injury* to the saints. The word "injurious" in this verse comes from the word *hubris* meaning "to injure with pleasure." It speaks of a violence characterized by an inhumane spirit. Not until Christ arrested him on Damascus Road and quickened his heart was Paul's mad campaign to rid the world of Christians suspended.

Likewise, the people who heard Stephen's sermon, recorded in Acts 7, expressed more than a mere passive disagreement to his sermon. Instead, they *"gnashed on him with their teeth"* (Acts 7:54) and stoned him to death outside the city gates.

This is the kind of active hostility and religious extremism with which Jesus met from the Pharisees of his day. Further, this level of animosity is closely akin to the kind of anti-christian hatred displayed by the devil himself. In verses 38-41a and 44, Jesus identifies his persecutors as the devil's children by imitation. Their murderous design against the Son of God and their violent opposition to his truth resembles the devices of Satan and identifies them with him instead of Abraham (cf. 1 Jno. 3:10). It is in this sense of "imitation," not spiritual procreation, that unregenerate sinners are identified as "children of the devil" in the Bible. By nature, every unregenerate person *"walks according to the prince of the power of the air, the spirit that now worketh in the children of disobedience"* (Eph. 2:3).

Another characteristic of the unregenerate sinner is **spiritual inability**: *"Why do ye not understand my speech? Even because ye cannot hear my word...He that is of God heareth God's words: ye therefore hear them not, because ye are not of God"* (vs. 43, 48). Note the word *"cannot"* which speaks of inability. The natural man, i.e. apart from the grace of regeneration, is spiritually incapacitated. Because he is *"dead in trespasses and in sins"* (Eph. 2:1), he doesn't have the capacity to understand

148

and receive spiritual truth (cf. 1 Cor. 2:14; Rom. 8:7; Jno. 6:44; Jer. 13:23). Jeremiah 6:10 clearly describes the condition of man by nature: *"To whom shall I speak, and give warning, that they may hear? Behold, their ear is uncircumcised, and they cannot hearken: behold, the word of the Lord is unto them a reproach; they have no delight in it."*

It is only the individual who belongs to God in a vital relationship that can hear God's words (v. 48). Indeed, the natural man may hear the audible sound, but he cannot discern the spiritual message. He may hear and rationally process the argument by means of his physical ear, but it will not touch his heart or mean anything to him in his soul. Before a person can hear and receive spiritual truth, he must have *"ears to hear."* Such spiritual ability is the gift of God (cf. Rev. 3:6,13,22; Pro. 20:12).

Christ, Greater than Abraham (vs. 51-59)

"If a man keep my saying, he shall never see death" (v. 51). The final chapter in this lengthy debate with the Pharisees is prefaced by yet another claim by Jesus that the religious leaders deemed incredible (cf. vs. 12, 32). In this passage, as in 11:26, Jesus speaks of death in its ultimate sense, i.e. final and eternal death. That a disciple of Christ, because he gives evidence by his discipleship that he is a child of God, will never finally and ultimately die is a blessed truth (cf. Rev. 20:6).

These Pharisees, once again however, cannot think beyond the physical, material and natural realm of the senses. *"Now we know that thou hast a devil. Abraham is dead, and the prophets...art thou greater than our father Abraham, which is dead? And the prophets are dead: whom makest thou thyself?"* (vs. 52-53). Their question exposes the contempt and scorn they harbored against Jesus. Greater than Abraham? No doubt, they thought that this claim would be the death knell to his credibility. This time, he would not escape the consequences of such a preposterous claim.

Surely Jesus would not claim superiority to the father of the Jews, would he? In fact, he would and he did. His superiority to Abraham is based on two great facts: (1) Jesus is the fulfillment of the Abrahamic Covenant; (2) Jesus is the Son of God.

(1) Jesus is the fulfillment of the Abrahamic Covenant. He is Abraham's "seed," the One in whom God promised Abraham that he would bless "all the families of the earth" (cf. Gal. 3:16). Jesus responded *"Your father Abraham rejoiced to see my day: and he saw it, and was glad"* (v. 56).

When did Abraham see Christ's day? He saw it when he took Isaac atop Mount Moriah to offer him as a sacrifice (cf. Gen. 22). On that occasion, Isaac was spared and the "ram caught by his horns in a thicket" was offered in Isaac's stead. He named that place "Jehovah-jireh" because, as he said, "In the mount of the Lord it shall be seen."

150

One might ask *"what* shall be seen"? The means by which "God would provide himself a lamb for the sacrifice" shall be seen. Abraham saw God's provision for sinners in the substitutionary sacrifice on Moriah. According to Hebrews 11:17-19, he saw Christ "in a figure" that day, and he rejoiced and was glad. He saw Christ "by faith," if you please – the same way that believers now see Him and are glad.

(2) Jesus is the Son of God. When the Jews retorted that he was not yet fifty years old and Abraham had been dead for many centuries, Jesus replies *"Before Abraham was I am"* (v. 56).

Jesus is claiming preexistence to Abraham. But he is claiming more than that. He is claiming eternally present preexistence to Abraham. He does not say, merely, "Before Abraham was, I was." That would be preexistence. Instead, he says, "Before Abraham was, I am"—present tense! This is a most amazing claim and one that could only be interpreted in terms of a claim to Deity.

Did the Jews understand that he was equating himself to Jehovah? Indeed they did, for they *"took up stones to cast at him."* Blasphemers deserved to be stoned under the law. Anyone that undeservingly took God's sacred name deserved to die. But Jesus deserved to be praised, for he was, and is, the great "I am."

Chapter 14
Living in Liberty (John 9)

John 9 records the sixth of seven miracles highlighted in John's Gospel as evidence of the divine nature of Jesus—the restoration of sight to the man who was born blind. In each of these seven signs (or miracles), Jesus demonstrates his divine sovereignty—this time, his sovereignty over darkness. He who is "the light of the world" (v. 5) dispelled the darkness of this man who was born blind and so, transformed his life. John is the only evangelist who records this particular episode from Jesus' ministry.

The narrative of John 9 follows on the heels of the adversarial exchange with the Pharisees in chapter 8, forming a stark contrast between the legalistic bondage that characterized the religious rulers among the Jews and the spiritual freedom that Jesus Christ brings to the lives of his disciples. The narrative may be divided into three sections: (1) Light (vs. 1-12); Legalism (vs. 13-23); Liberty (vs. 24-41). Before working our way through the story, however, consider that this account is a poignant picture of God's grace in the salvation of sinners.

A Picture of Grace

It is worth noting that this chapter is a wonderful illustration of salvation by grace alone. Notice that the man was born with this defect (v. 2), just as sinners are born fallen and depraved (cf. Ps. 51:5).

Note secondly that he does not appeal to Jesus for help, but Jesus takes the initiative to move toward him with unsolicited and voluntary kindness (vs. 1-7). Even so, man by nature is the beneficiary, not the sponsor, of God's gracious initiative in salvation. Left to himself, the fallen sinner would never seek God (cf. Rom. 3:11). It is the Shepherd that finds the lost sheep, not man that finds the Lord (cf. Deut. 32:10; Lk. 19:10).

Note, in the third place, that this man had done nothing to merit such gracious attention. There was no obligation on Jesus to intervene. The favor bestowed upon him was completely free and voluntary. Even so, the God of grace acts in kindness upon undeserving sinners to bless them in spite of their lack of merit.

Fourthly, the blessing bestowed upon this man transformed his life. For the first time ever, he could see. He could see sunsets, and flowers, and the faces of other people. Imagine his joy and gladness to finally experience his world beyond the sense of mere hearing. No longer was he beholden to others for his daily subsistence. Now he could work, and travel, and enjoy his world at a previously unrealized level.

So, God's gift of grace to sinners is life-changing. Now the new-born babe can enjoy the sincere milk of the word (cf. 1

Pet. 2:2). Now he has the ability to "see and enter God's kingdom" (Jno. 3:3,5). Now he has the capacity to understand spiritual things (cf. 1 Cor. 2:14) and to function in a realm beyond the purely natural and carnal.

Light (vs. 1-12)

The healing of this blind man illustrates our Lord's claim in John 8:12, *"I am the light of the world,"* a claim he now repeats in verse 5: *"As long as I am in the world, I am the light of the world."* Though this poor man had lived in complete darkness since the day of his birth, Jesus brought light into his life.

We've encountered this light/darkness motif previously in John's Gospel. In the prologue, John traces the source of all light to the life of God the Word: *"In him was life; and the life was the light of men. And the light shineth in darkness; and the darkness comprehended it not"* (1:4-5). Then, he identifies John the Baptist as one who pointed men to that "true Light" that followed him: *"The same came for a witness, to bear witness of the Light...He was not that Light, but was sent to bear witness of that Light. That was the true Light, which lighteth every man that cometh into the world"* (1:7a, 8-9).

The true Light! What a sublime title given to the Lord Jesus Christ! Jesus alone can dispel the darkness in the hearts and lives of men.

Of course, everyone does not appreciate the Light. The Pharisees whose animosity toward Christ was so evident in the previous chapter (cf. 8:12-59) rebelled against the light of truth and resented Jesus for exposing their hypocrisy. Their resistance and opposition to Jesus is an example of the principle expressed earlier in John 3:19-20: *"And this is the condemnation, that light is come into the world, and men loved darkness rather than light, because their deeds were evil. For every one that doeth evil hateth the light, neither cometh to the light, lest his deeds should be reproved."*

In the Bible, light stands as a metaphor for truth, knowledge, understanding, and purity. Darkness, on the other hand, represents ignorance, confusion, and sin. By a miracle of healing the man born blind, Jesus both bestows a kindness upon this man as an individual and gives evidence of his identity as the true Light of the world.

It is true that there is some light to be found in science and philosophy and education, but even that light ultimately derives from nature's Creator God. Voltaire, Rousseau, Kant and other 18th century Enlightenment philosophers insisted that human reason could liberate humanity from the ignorance of superstition, and while their theories contributed to the economic and social progress of the industrial revolution, still they did not resolve the deep darkness of human exploitation, the bondage of addiction, or the problems of relational strife and conflict in the world. Only Jesus Christ can dispel the darkness that is in the human heart.

Legalism (vs. 13-23)

The people quickly recognized a change in this man. After learning that he was, in fact, the same man they had long witnessed begging for money, they asked him how he was now able to see. He replied that a man named Jesus opened his eyes (vs. 8-10).

Soon, the Pharisees heard the news and summoned the man for questioning. Without hesitation, he testified to the facts of his transformation. Though they couldn't dispute the miracle that had taken place, the Pharisees were concerned that the wrong inference concerning Jesus would not be deduced. "Don't read too much into this situation," they seem to say. *"This man is not of God, because he keepeth not the Sabbath day"* (v. 16). The man testified his conviction, however, that Jesus was *"a prophet"* (v. 17).

The Pharisee's religion was all about keeping the rules. To them, rules were even more important than people. They were the legal watchdogs—the self-appointed hawks of orthodoxy.

Jesus, however, was more concerned about people than keeping man-made rules. His was a ministry of mercy. He came to bind up the wounded, liberate the captives, and lift up the downcast (cf. Lk 4:18); consequently, the Lord Jesus met with conflict at every turn from the legalists of the day.

Legalism is a subtle and insidious evil. Although it is encouraging to witness someone become serious enough about serving the Lord that he begins to regulate and discipline his own behavior, it is sad to see that same person adopt a judgmental posture and attitude of rigidity toward others. Once a person feels that he has arrived at some level of perfection, and proceeds to impose his conscience as the standard by which the righteousness of others is measured, he has fallen precariously into the subtle trap of the legalist.

Legalism is all about control. Almost all cults, especially the religious ones, depend on a legalistic structure for the sake of policing its members. It dawned on me recently that a legalist defines "sin" in narrow terms, sets out to master that particular "sin," then imposes this narrow definition upon others as the standard by which he judges and seeks to control them.

The legalist says "You are righteous if you don't eat pork," or don't dance, or don't smoke, or don't watch television, or don't have a tattoo, or don't eat processed sugar, or have never been divorced, or don't take anti-depressants, etc. Or we might frame it in positive terms: "You are righteous if you regularly tithe," or homeschool your children, or have no debt, or wear neutral colors, or control your weight, or grow and process your own food, etc. The possibilities are endless; furthermore, the problem is that once the controllee achieves mastery over whatever particular "sin" has been identified as "mortal" and unpardonable, the controller redefines the parameters to include further behaviors that are likewise essential if an individual is to achieve perfection.

Of course, it needs to be said that there is such a thing as "sin." But it is also true that God defines what is "sin" in His word and pledges to adjudicate the case of each person righteously. The legalist, however, inevitably presumes to narrow that definition to a particular behavior (or set of behaviors), using his own self-mastery in that area to pass judgment on others, and effectively wrests the gavel from the hand of God. "I've figured out the secret," he (she) boasts, "and if you want to be perfect like me then you must submit to my authority."

There are few forms of bondage quite as dangerous as legalism. Perhaps that explains the fact that both the Lord Jesus and the apostle Paul saved their harshest words and most strident denunciations for the legalists of their day. If you've ever been exposed to the tactics of a controller (either an aggressive one, or a passive-aggressive one), you likely have a window into the motive behind David's prayer, "Let me not fall into the hands of men, but let me fall into the hand of the Lord, for He is merciful."

Pharisaism in Jesus' day was the epitome of this principle of "good gone wrong." This Jewish sect began during the Babylonian captivity (~600 B.C.) with a group of loyalists committed to making sure that the true worship of God was not lost while the Jews were in Babylon. By the time of Jesus, however, their legitimate concern for the integrity of God's word and the glory of God's name had degenerated into a

159

caricature of orthodoxy marked by man-made rules and traditions.

One such tradition concerned safeguards they implemented to protect the sanctity of the Sabbath. In the Mosaic Law, God prohibited manual labor on the Sabbath day. Eager to codify that prohibition in very detailed and practical terms, however, the Pharisees had embellished the Divine prohibition to include practically every exertion of physical energy. They even had a law against kneading dough on the Sabbath.

Of course, it was a Sabbath day when Jesus restored sight to the man born blind. And in the process, he had spat upon the ground, made clay of the spittle, and anointed the eyes of the blind man with the clay (v. 6). When the Pharisees realized that this healing miracle had taken place on the Sabbath, they set out to investigate the details to see if perhaps Jesus had failed to comply with the technicalities of "the law" (vs. 13-14). Could it be, they wondered, that Jesus had violated their prohibition against kneading dough when he fabricated a plaster from clay?

Stop and ask yourself at this point if it is really possible that Jesus had sinned by making clay, anointing the blind man's eyes, and restoring his sight on the Sabbath day. The very idea sounds preposterous to those of us looking at the situation from the distance of two thousand years, and rightly so. But the Pharisees really believed that Jesus had committed a great sin: *"Therefore said some of the Pharisees, This man is not*

160

of God, because he keepeth not the sabbath day. Others said, How can a man that is a sinner do such miracles? And there was a division among them" (9:16). This is legalism run amok. In their zeal to protect the rules (which they really thought were God's rules), they found it impossible to rejoice with the man who could now see for the first time in his life.

So, the Pharisees proceeded to investigate the situation. It is clear that they are in full, damage-control mode. They asked the blind man for his interpretation of the event (v. 16), but they had already concluded that this was not a legitimate miracle. The only possible option remaining was that the man was just pretending to be blind: *"But the Jews did not believe concerning him, that he had been blind, and received his sight"* (v. 18a). So, they summoned the parents (v. 18b) and asked, *"Is this your son, who ye say was born blind? How then doth he now see?"* (v. 19).

How sad is the reply from his parents! Instead of rejoicing at this amazing miracle that has touched their precious child, the parents caved in fear before the council: *"We know that this is our son, and that he was born blind: but by what means he now seeth, we know not; or who hath opened his eyes, we know not: he is of age; ask him: he shall speak for himself"* (vs. 20-21). Verse 22 explains the parents' cowardice in terms of the threat of excommunication: *"These words spake his parents, because they feared the Jews: for the Jews had agreed already, that if any man did confess that he was Christ, he should be put out of the synagogue."*

161

Legalism is an ugly religion that controls people by intimidation and fear.

Liberty (vs. 24-41)

Again, the Pharisees called the man born blind, attempting to enforce an official, theological interpretation of the event: *"Give God the praise: we know that this man is a sinner"* (v. 25). But the blind man refuses to comply: *"Whether he be a sinner or no, I know not: one thing I know not: one thing I know, that whereas I was blind, now I see"* (v. 26). This man knows that he is not what he used to be and he cannot deny the transformation that has occurred in his life.

"One thing I know..." We may learn from this that the individual whose life has been transformed by Jesus may not initially understand much about what has happened. He is frequently unable to adequately interpret the change that has taken place in theological terms, or to fully comprehend the implications of it all. All he knows is the simple fact that *"Whereas I was blind, now I see"* (v. 25). That experiential reality, however, is beyond dispute, regardless of the strong-arm tactics of the legalists to control the narrative.

The man born blind refuses to live in the intimidation and fear of legalism. He may not possess the same ability as these religious professionals to frame the event in theological categories, but he refuses to permit them to minimize his experience. His life has been so radically altered for the better that, even though he cannot explain everything that has happened—even though his theology is not yet refined and informed, and even though his knowledge is immature and partial—he cannot deny the blessing he has experienced.

An experience of grace is a powerful incentive to live in liberty. This individual, whose life has been so remarkably changed by the Lord Jesus, knows that he is not what he used to be, and that knowledge—basic and elementary as it is—is enough to give him amazing courage to stand up against these religious bullies.

That courageous spirit is evident in the matter-of-fact, unashamed witness recorded in verses 26-34. By this point, the man born blind has begun to see that their motives are less than sincere. When they ask again, *"How opened he thine eyes?"*, he replies, *"I have told you already, and ye did not hear: wherefore would ye hear it again? Will ye also be his disciples?"* (vs. 26-27). The very idea that he might push back at their unwillingness to consider the facts triggers these religious leaders: *"Then they reviled him, and said, Thou art his disciple; but we are Moses' disciples. We know that God spake unto Moses: as for this fellow, we know not from whence he is"* (vs. 28-29).

The liberated man, however, still refuses to cower before their insults, but offers them his own theological explanation: *"Why herein is a marvellous thing, that ye know not from whence he is, and yet he hath opened mine eyes. Now we know that God heareth not sinners: but if any man be a worshipper of God, and doeth his will, him he heareth. Since the world began was it not heard that any man opened the eys of one that was born blind. If this man were not of God, he could do nothing"* (vs. 30-33).

His impertinence in daring to advance an opinion on the identity of Jesus was too much for the Pharisees. They responded with an *ad hominem* attack exposing the real animosity of their hearts: *"Thou wast altogether born in sins, and dost thou teach us?"* (v. 34). "How dare this substandard person (whose native handicap proved his inferiority) presume to teach righteous and important people like us!" they retort. Now, we see their true colors shining through. *"And they cast him out"* of the synagogue, excommunicating him for his insolence (v. 34b).

Indeed, there is little place in religious legalism for someone that lives in liberty. But unlike his parents who feared excommunication more than anything else, he refused to permit these sourpuss theologians with their wrinkled brows of concern to shackle his joy in the Lord. And though his refusal to play the legalist's game cost him what little reputation he once thought himself to possess in their eyes (which, evidently, was not very much at all), it was a sacrifice worth making, for he soon found a warm welcome among the followers of Jesus (cf. vs. 35-38).

As previously noted, John 9 is a commentary on John 8, both in terms of the reference to Jesus as the Light of the world (8:12; 9:5) and in terms of the militant animosity of those whose religion is all about self-righteousness and pride (8:13ff; 9:13-34). But it is also a commentary on Jesus' teaching

164

concerning spiritual freedom and liberty: *"Ye shall know the truth, and the truth shall make you free...If the Son therefore shall make you free, ye shall be free indeed"* (8:32, 36). The man born blind discovered that spiritual freedom in the truth of God's amazing grace in Jesus Christ. He found an understanding of what had happened to him and embraced the gospel of grace as the only message that suited his case. And he found a home among those who lived in liberty.

How wonderful it is to see someone whose life has been transformed by the grace of God now brought to a greater understanding of the Savior and a readiness to follow the Lord Jesus Christ! How thrilling to see a little child of God emancipated from the bondage of legalism!

Chapter 15
The Parable of the Good Shepherd (John 10)

John 10 contains the only parable (v. 6) in John's Gospel[1], i.e. the parable of the Good Shepherd and his sheep. The blessed reality suggested in this parable is the intimate relationship between, and the tender care and sacrificial commitment of, the Shepherd to his sheep.

John 10 is the New Testament version of Psalm 23 and the Lord Jesus Christ is the John 10 parallel to the Jehovah in the 23rd Psalm. Here is, therefore, another evidence in John's Gospel to the claim that Jesus is God of very God.

This discourse follows on the heels of the closing comments of chapter 9. The Pharisees claimed to be the guides of the people. But Jesus accused them of blindness (cf. 9:39-41). Now he claims to be the true Shepherd and Guide of his people, and contrasts his commitment to them against the Pharisees, whom he compares to thieves and hirelings. This contrast between false shepherds who fleeced the flock and Jehovah's faithful commitment to shepherd and care for his own is a familiar motif in the Old Testament (cf. Eze. 34; Jer. 23:1-6; Is. 56:8-12).

---

[1] A parable is a story used to illustrate a reality.

Jesus draws from familiar imagery in this parable. An Eastern "sheepfold" was common property in the community. Each village had a place protected by a large wall where various shepherds might keep their respective flocks to protect them from nightly predatory dangers. When the sheep passed through the "door" (or gate) into the sheepfold, they were committed into the care of a porter whose job it was to stand guard against thieves and wolves during the night. When the next morning dawned, the various shepherds would return to call their sheep. The sheep would respond to the voice of their shepherd and he would, subsequently, lead them out to pasture.

This is the well-known image our Lord develops in verses 1-5 to describe the difference between himself and the religious leaders among the Jews. The Pharisees, he claims, were not truly committed to the people. They were *"thieves and robbers"* (v. 1) and *"strangers"* (v. 5). And the people did not respond positively to their hard rules and regulations. The sheep were afraid of these hireling shepherds who had gained access by unlawful means (v. 1).

Unlike these imposters, however, Jesus had *"entered by the door"* (v. 2), i.e. lawfully and legitimately, according to God's holy law. He fulfilled Messianic prophecy, and conformed to everything that the law required. He is the true Shepherd (v. 2).

"To him the porter openeth" (v. 3a). This obviously refers to John the Baptist, who presented the Lord Jesus to the people, like a forerunner announces a coming king (cf. 1:31).

"...and the sheep hear his voice..." (v. 3b). The true Shepherd enters the sheepfold lawfully, is identified by the porter, and is recognized by his sheep. When Jesus came preaching *"Blessed are the poor in spirit, for theirs is the kingdom of heaven,"* his message resonated in the hearts of the people. *"The common people,"* burdened down under the heavy yoke of legalism for so long, *"heard him gladly"* (cf. Mr. 12:37).

John 10:1-5 is really a commentary on the account of the Blind Beggar in John 9. Not only had the religious leaders among the Jews not helped this blind man, but they had also dealt harshly and condescendingly with him after Jesus healed him. Jesus had entered the door of the sheepfold, as it were, lawfully, for he had come working the works of God (9:4). Like a good Shepherd, he had sought ought this little lamb of the fold and cared for his needs. In response, the blind man had recognized the voice of the Shepherd and responded to it. The hard conditions of the Pharisees, however, did not resonate with his needs. Clearly, Jesus had demonstrated that he is the true Shepherd and that the Pharisees had acted as strangers, thieves, and robbers.

Though the Pharisees excommunicated the blind man from the temple and cut him off from safety and blessing (as they thought), Jesus had given to him true safety and blessing in His own sheepfold. Unlike the Pharisees who used people for themselves, the Good Shepherd would not harm the sheep, but would instead give His own life for their welfare and safety (v. 11). How blessed are they who are under the faithful care and provision of the Good Shepherd, the Lord and Savior Jesus Christ!

Thieves and Robbers

The meaning of our Lord's parable contrasting the Jewish religious leaders, who were thieves and robbers, with himself, the true Shepherd, was lost on the Pharisees (v. 6). They failed to grasp the connection he made to Old Testament imagery regarding the "false shepherds" that had misused the Lord's flock and the Lord's commitment to care for them himself (cf. Eze. 34). So Jesus changes the image slightly to make the same point.

"Then Jesus said unto them again, Verily, verily, I say unto you, I am the door of the sheep. All that ever came before me are thieves and robbers: but the sheep did not hear them. I am the door: by me if any man enter in, he shall be saved, and shall go in and out, and find pasture" (vs. 7-9). The point of his parable in vs. 1-5 was to show that he had demonstrated his identity as the true Shepherd and that he, therefore, had the right to minister to God's covenant people. His point in vs 7-9 is to show that he alone, not the Pharisees, was committed to the flock and would lead them to blessing.

"I am the door of the sheep," in contrast to the thieves and robbers that preceded him. Just as a shepherd is the means by

which pasture and rest and safety and every other blessing is opened to the sheep, so Jesus Christ is the means of all blessing and salvation to God's little children.

"The thief cometh not, but for to steal, and to kill, and to destroy: I am come that they might have life, and that they might have it more abundantly" (v. 10). The contrast between "evil shepherds" (to whom our Lord here refers to as "thieves") and himself, the good Shepherd, is again highlighted in verse 10. The religious leaders were not true shepherds, Jesus argues. They did not have the interest of the flock at heart. Instead, they had insinuated themselves into this position of leadership and were using their position for personal privilege, even at the expense of the people. On the other hand, Jesus was committed to the welfare of the flock. He came to benefit them. He alone cares for them, protects them, and labors to improve their lot.

It is proper for Bible students to identify "the thief" in verse 10 as Satan, for the devil is the ultimate "thief." The very practice of exploiting human beings for personal advantage was invented by him, the original Demagogue.[2]

The devil *steals, kills,* and *destroys.* He takes that which does not belong to him and renders it useless. He will rob a person of his right mind. How many people have been prejudiced against the truth of Christ by the devil's lies? How many have lost their minds to drug or alcohol abuse? He robs people of

---

[2] A demagogue is a leader who gains personal power by championing the cause of the common people; one who exploits people for personal privilege.

the precious gift of time. Many have spent their lives running around in aimless circles, squandering the best years of life chasing fool's gold because they have been duped by the devil.

How many have lost their health because of indulgence in some ungodly activity? How many marriages have been trashed on the garbage heap of history because of infidelity or unresolved anger? How many lives that could have been lived productively to the glory of God have been sidetracked by the devil's deception, temptations, and assaults? Everywhere one may see people who are caught up in the "rat race," who walk according to the course of this world, who pursue the illusion of happiness and safety and security in things or recreation or money. This is nothing but that old thief the Devil, stealing hearts and lives away from the blessings that are available to them in the kingdom of God.

The Good Shepherd

In contrast, the Lord Jesus Christ came, not to fleece but, to feed the flock. He came to minister, to serve, to bless. He came *"that they might have life,"* i.e. eternal life, or life in the ultimate sense. Because of his death, his sheep will never die: *"For the wages of sin is death, but the gift of God is eternal life through Jesus Christ our Lord"* (Rom. 6:23). By means of his death, he has delivered them from *"so great a death,"* i.e. eternal separation from God (2 Cor. 1:10). On them, the second death exercises no power or authority (cf. Rev. 20:6). He *"tasted death"* for his own (Heb. 2:9) and thereby, brought death to death on their behalf.

But he is not only interested in their eternal, but also in their temporal welfare: *"...and that they might have it more abundantly."* Life *"more abundant"* refers to something over and above, or superlative (Greek *perissos*). "What could be over and above eternal life?" one questions. Nothing in terms of quality, but something in terms of quantity. In other words, something additional; something more. In addition to the reality of future blessedness, the Lord Jesus has purchased for his sheep the additional blessing of temporal fellowship with God and the experience of a bit of heaven this side of heaven in the fellowship of the church. What a good Shepherd is our Savior!

Verses 11-18 expand on the thought in verse 10, that is, the thought concerning **the good Shepherd's commitment to the welfare of his flock**. The contrast between Christ and the religious leaders of the Jews continues in this section of the parable. He is still "the good Shepherd." The religious leaders have previously been referred to as *"strangers"* (v. 5), *"thieves and robbers"* (vs. 1, 8); now, he refers to them as *"hirelings"* (vs. 12, 13).

A "hireling" is one who has no personally vested interested in the flock. He has been hired to superintend them temporarily while the shepherd attends to other, pressing business. The hireling has no guarantee of future employment. This temporary job, therefore, is simply a means of earning a bit of extra money.

Because a hireling's motives are self-centered, he tends to bail out when the going gets tough. He is more concerned about himself and his own safety than he is the safety of the flock over which he has been given responsibility. At the first sign of a predator or a band of sheep thieves, the hireling opts for self-protection.

By comparing the scribes and Pharisees to hirelings, our Lord highlights the fact that their desire to lead the people did not arise from an interest in the people, but rather, a concern for themselves. They were motivated by prestige and a position of influence. It was personal ambition, not love for the Lord's humble poor, that motivated them. He also pinpoints their lack of commitment to the welfare of the flock. When the wolf comes, the hireling will leave the sheep and flee because he doesn't care for them (vs. 12-13).

This passage has been properly used to discourage professionalism in gospel ministry. When preachers begin to see the ministry as a job or a career and make decisions regarding pastoral ministry on the basis of compensation packages, they violate the very tone and tenor of what it means to shepherd the flock of God.

Peter exhorted the elders to *"take the oversight of the flock, nor for filthy lucre, but of a ready mind"* (1 Pet. 5:2). Paul modeled this appropriate motivation in leadership, as 1 Corinthians 9:17-18 indicates: *"For if I do this thing willingly, I have a reward: but if against my will, a dispensation of the gospel is committed unto me. What is my reward then? Verily that, when I preach the gospel, I may make the gospel of Christ without charge, that I abuse not my power in the gospel."*

Primitive Baptist ministers have historically been bi-vocational, i.e. maintaining some form of secular employment or trade while serving in the pastoral ministry. Within the past three decades, a number of our ministers have been able to serve in a full-time pastoral capacity. I have been blessed to serve full-time for the past thirty-five years. During that time, however, I have learned by experience that it takes two primary things for such an arrangement to succeed: (1) A congregation that is sufficiently sizeable and financially solvent to support a pastor and his family; (2) A pastor that is willing to labor and not become lazy.

There is a subtle danger associated with full-time ministry. It is the peril of beginning to think of the pastorate as a job and the stipend as an entitlement. Professionalism in ministry, in other words, is an easy trap and it is not difficult for a minister to unwittingly develop the mindset of a "hireling."

In contrast to the professional preachers of his day, our Lord is truly committed to the flock. He lays down his life for the sheep (v. 11). In every respect, he considers their well-being above his own comfort. Their safety takes precedence over his own ease and enjoyment.

Further, he is intimately acquainted with them. He *"knows"* his sheep, as verse 14 indicates. He knows their various traits and characteristics. His eye sees every developing problem, whether a developing limp in a ewe over there or tension between two rams over here. He knows the personality of each and works to make them comfortable and healthy. This intimate relationship between Shepherd and flock is an extension of the loving relationship between the Father and the Son (v. 15).

Also, the Lord Jesus Christ, the true Shepherd, is interested in the entire flock. Jesus' reference to *"other sheep...which are not of this fold"* is a reference to the Gentiles. His current followers consisted of Jews only. But he also has people that belong to him among the Gentiles and here, he expresses his intention to bring them into the gospel fold.

He concludes the parable by stating that his commitment to lay down his life on behalf of his sheep is a voluntary commitment. So vested is he in their final happiness and security that he willingly sacrifices himself to win their eternal security (vs. 17-18). With such a Shepherd and Bishop of our souls, what have we to fear?

A Rhapsody of Sovereign Grace (vs. 19-30)

Once again, as verses 19-21 indicate, public opinion was divided over the true identity of Jesus. Some said *"He hath a devil"* and others, *"Can a devil open the eyes of the blind?"*, a reference no doubt to the recent event recorded in John 9. Public opinion is never a good criteria for determining truth. Just because an idea is popular or unpopular, whatever the case may be, is not a good benchmark for measuring its legitimacy. The majority is seldom right.

Jesus' parabolic message on "the Shepherd and his sheep" was delivered at Jerusalem during the Feast of Dedication (vs. 22). *"It was winter,"* comments John, and we can almost feel the chill in the air as opposition to Jesus mounts among the Jewish rulers. The truths revealed in verses 26-30, however, tend to warm the hearts of sensible sinners. This passage is a veritable rhapsody of sovereign grace.

The Jews approached him again in Solomon's porch (v. 23) and urged him to tell them plainly whether or not He is the Christ (v. 24). He answered, *"I told you, and ye believed not: the works that I do in my Father's name, they bear witness of me"* (v. 25). Once more, he appeals to the seven signs, or miracles, as evidence of His Messianic identity as the Son of God. They, however, did not believe. He now proceeds to state several glorious truths, the first of which explains the reason for their unbelief.

(1) **Total Depravity**: *"But ye believe not because ye are not of my sheep"* (v. 26). Here he describes the unresponsiveness of natural men to spiritual truth. Note that Jesus did not say "You are not of my sheep because you don't believe." Such a statement would imply that the act of believing in Jesus is necessary in order to belong to him. Instead, he taught that a person must first belong to him before he is capable of believing.

177

Though there are other reasons cited in the Scriptures that explain why a person might disbelieve in Jesus, the first and most basic is "total depravity," or the inability of the fallen nature to believe (cf. 1 Cor. 2:14; Jno. 8:43). Faith is the fruit of the Spirit (Gal. 5:22) and until a person has been quickened into new life, he does not have the ability to believe. Of course, only those who belong to God by electing grace will be born of the Spirit (cf. Rom. 8:29-30; Acts 13:48); hence, a person must belong to God as one of His sheep before he has the capacity to believe.

(2) *Effectual Calling*: "*My sheep hear my voice, and I know them, and they follow me*" (v. 27). When the Lord speaks the life giving voice to the objects of his eternal love, they hear and respond. Note the expression "*I know them.*" This speaks of the covenant relationship (or relational love)—the theological term is "foreknowledge"—between the Shepherd and his sheep. He loved them before time began. When he calls them, therefore, they hear him (cf. Jno. 5:25) and are drawn to him irresistibly. This is the meaning of the clause "*and they follow me.*"

(3) *Divine Preservation*: "*I give unto them eternal life and they shall never perish*" (v. 28). The language of this verse is very particular and definite. I give unto "*them*," that is, the sheep, "*eternal life.*" Jesus came to give, not to offer, eternal life to a particular people. What people was that? Those that were given to him by the Father: "*My Father which gave them me...*" (v. 29a). And those to whom He gives eternal life will "*never*

178

perish." They are eternally secure, preserved in the Good Shepherd's sovereign hand.

No man is able to pluck the sheep from the Shepherd's hand (v. 28). How wonderful is the doctrine of the Divine preservation of the saints! The sheep are guarded well by their Good Shepherd. He will not lose one to the roaring lion.

(4) *The Sovereignty of God:* "*My Father...is greater than all... I and my Father are one*" (vs. 29-30). God is almighty over all. None can rival or oppose Him. The final safety and security of the sheep depends not on their performance and perseverance but upon the sovereign power of God. The salvation of sinners is the work of the Holy Trinity working in unison (v. 30), and it is protected and secured by that same Holy Trinity (cf. Col. 3:1-4). With such a message of sovereign grace, we may indeed feel our hearts to be strangely warmed, even in the coldest of winters here below.

The Charge of Blasphemy (10:31-42)

On the heels of Jesus' claim of essential union with God the Father (v. 30), the "*Jews took up stones again to stone him*" (v. 31). Stoning, of course, was the prescribed punishment for blasphemy (cf. Lev. 24:14-16).

We see here that the antagonism to Jesus has now reached a point of hostility. The threat of physical harm against him is now very real.

Before the first stone is hurled, however, Jesus appeals in the cause of his own innocence: "*Many good works have I*

179

showed you from my Father; for which of those works do ye stone me?" (v. 32). He had healed the sick, cleansed the lepers, and fed the multitude. These works of benevolence had promoted the happiness and comfort of men. What had he done that was worthy of death? Like Daniel before him, the Lord Jesus could only be charged in things pertaining to the worship of God. Would to God that could be said of every believer!

They replied, *"For a good work we stone thee not; but for blasphemy; and because thou, being a man, makest thyself God"* (v. 33). The charge of blasphemy would eventually be the official indictment from Caiaphas and the Sanhedrin that warranted his crucifixion. They would tell Pilate *"We have a law and by our law he ought to die because he made himself the Son of God"* (Jno. 19:7). But interestingly, the Law did not prescribe death by means of crucifixion for blasphemers, but death by stoning. So in their pretended concern for the "law," they themselves would violate it.

Our Lord replies to their appeal to the law as proof that he was a blasphemer by quoting from that law: *"Is it not written in your law, I said, Ye are gods? If he called them gods, unto whom the word of God came, and the Scripture cannot be broken; say ye of him, whom the Father hath sanctified and sent into the world, Thou blasphemest; because I said, I am the Son of God?"* (vs. 34-36). His argument here is interesting. He quotes from Psalm 82:6 where God inspired the Psalmist to write of public officials as "gods" in order to describe the dignity of the office they hold. Jesus is saying, essentially, "If God himself in the Scripture

180

uses the word 'god' to describe magistrates and judges, then it is right and proper to use the word to speak of people in places of authority. It cannot be blasphemy, then, to apply the term to the Messiah, someone who is even in a more exalted position than magistrates."

Verse 36 describes the Messiah as the One "*whom the Father hath sanctified and sent into the world.*" When was the Messiah "set apart" to this office? He was "set apart" in the covenant of grace before the foundation of the world. Then God asked, "*Whom shall I send and who will go for us?*" The Son of God answered, "*Here am I, send me*" (Is. 6:8). Then in the fullness of the time, God sent forth his Son (Gal. 4:4). Just as judges and magistrates spoke with the authority of Jehovah in olden times, so the Messiah essentially represented the Father when he came into the world. The office of Mediator was far more exalted than that of magistrates.

This debunking of the charge of blasphemy did not satisfy the madness of the Jewish rulers. They still sought to take him (v. 39), but again "*he escaped out of their hand and went*" once more to the place where his ministry began (v. 40). The fact that all of their plots and conspiracies were ineffective is another evidence of His divine character and the great truth that when he did, in fact, go to the cross, he went voluntarily, not because he was victimized by wicked men (cf. 10:18).

Chapter 16
In the Shadow of the Cross (John 11-12)

When we come to John chapters 11 and 12, we enter the final week of the earthly life and ministry of the Lord Jesus Christ. The events of this final week will take us through chapter 18, but for now we will consider the single event that raised the tension between Jesus and the Pharisees to a completely new level, i.e. the resurrection of Lazarus.

The Seventh Miracle (Jno. 11)

The seventh miracle in this "book of the seven signs" is the resurrection of Lazarus from the dead, as recorded in John 11. This miracle, more than any other, displays the Deity of the Lord Jesus Christ in that it demonstrates his sovereignty over death. Only God possesses authority over death. In demonstrating his power over death, Jesus demonstrates that he is, indeed, God manifest in the flesh.

It was because of this miracle that *"many Jews believed on him"* (cf. 12:11). Though the religious leaders sought to dismiss the other miracles as flukes or legends, they were unsuccessful in the effort to discredit this one. There is, after all, very little one can do to undercut the effect of a dead man brought back to life. It was this miracle, too, that brought the leaders to the decision to finally, once and for all, put an end to Jesus.

How wonderful to believe in a God that can raise the dead! How wonderful to trust a Christ who is himself *"the resurrection and the life!"* If he can conquer death, man's greatest enemy, then he can conquer every enemy we face in our lives. If he can solve our biggest problem, then there is no difficulty that the believer will face in his life too great for the Lord Jesus to resolve.

Not only does John 11 and the account of the resurrection of Lazarus give evidence for the Deity of Jesus, it also illustrates the life-giving power of the Lord Jesus Christ in terms of quickening the dead sinner to spiritual life. Notice that in the case of Lazarus, Jesus spoke directly to the dead without the use of media. His call was personal (*"Lazarus, come forth"*). His call was effectual (*"He that was dead came forth, bound hand and foot with grave clothes"*). And His call was direct and immediate. He did not ask the disciples to speak for Him. He did not send a message through some messenger. There was no human agency invoked and there was no voluntary cooperation from the deceased. Jesus spoke, by sovereign fiat, and it was done.

Jesus, on the contrary, did not always unstop the ears of the deaf, or give sight to the blind in the same way. To the blind man in John 9, Jesus made clay, anointed his eyes, and told him to go wash in the pool of Siloam. On another occasion, He healed the blind man in stages (Mr. 8:22ff). Each episode of resurrection recorded in the Gospels, however, occurred in precisely the same way. Jesus spoke. He spoke directly. He spoke personally. He spoke effectually. He spoke sovereignly. In the same way, Christ raises dead sinners to spiritual life. He speaks the life-giving voice, calling His own by name. The dead hear, and the dead live.

Furthermore, Jesus always went to the dead. The dead did not come to Him personally, neither were they brought to Him by some concerned friend or relative. He always went to the dead. The sick, the blind, and the palsied, on the contrary, were brought to Him.

In the work of raising dead sinners to life in Christ, the pattern is the same. The sinner does not come to Christ to get salvation. He is not brought to Christ by the prayers of some concerned friend or the efforts of some Christian worker. Christ goes to the sinner and meets him at the point of his need. He walks into the sepulcher of the depraved heart and breathes life into man's deadness and the sinner comes forth, Lazarus-like, into new life.

Once the dead sinner is raised to new life in Christ, the gospel serves to release that newborn soul from bondage. The preacher cannot raise Lazarus, but he can, once Christ has given him life, *"loose him and let him go.,"* as Jesus commanded his disciples (v. 44). This distinction between the work of the Lord and the work of the gospel minister is crucial. Only when one understands that he did not contribute toward his own salvation can he properly honor and glorify the Christ that saved him. God does everything necessary for salvation; therefore, He receives all the glory. From first to last, salvation is of the Lord.

One day, the same Christ will speak once more. He will issue the Divine imperative to all that are in the graves, and there will be a resurrection of the just and the unjust (cf. Jno. 5:28; Dan. 12:1-2; Acts 24:15). Those who have participated in the "first resurrection," that is the inward resurrection from death in sin to life in Christ, will not be touched by the "second death" (Rev. 20:6). But those who are still in an unregenerate and natural state will be raised to condemnation – to die an ultimate and final death, never to live again.

To trust in the "God that raiseth the dead," as Paul puts it in 2 Corinthians 1:9, is to put confidence in the Christ that *"hath delivered us from so great a death"* that he is further able to also deliver us even now, as well as at the last day (2 Cor. 1:8-10).

The Final Week of Jesus' Ministry (Jno. 12)

As opposition to Jesus from the religious leaders reached a fevered pitch and imperiled his safety, Jesus withdrew to the countryside for approximately six months (cf. 10:40). Lazarus' sickness, in which Mary & Martha sent for Jesus (cf. Jno. 11), occasioned a visit to the village of Bethany (about 2 miles from Jerusalem), and a return to public visibility. The subsequent fall-out of Lazarus' resurrection now made it virtually impossible for Jesus to maintain a "low profile" any longer.

The Lord knows that his time is at hand (cf. 12:23); hence, we come in Chapter 12 to the final week before the cross and Jesus' return to Bethany: *"Then Jesus six days before the Passover came to Bethany, where Lazarus was which had been dead, whom he raised from the dead. There they made him a supper; and Martha served: but Lazarus was one of them that sat at the table with him"* (vs. 1-2).

The house at which they met, according to the parallel passage in Mt. 26:6-13, is the house of Simon the leper, who was also a follower of Jesus. Why Martha served the meal at this man's house we are not told. Perhaps he was a widower, or bachelor who had no wife to play "hostess" to guests. Or perhaps Martha just naturally tended to assume such a role wherever she went. Interestingly, Martha is always depicted in the Gospels in the role of hostess or server, and her sister Mary is always pictured at Jesus' feet. It is no different on this occasion. Whatever the logistics, it is evident that Mary, Martha, Lazarus and Simon the leper knew each other and had a common interest in Jesus and his apostles.

Three particular characters stand out in this narrative.

Lazarus – A Living Wonder

The fact that Lazarus is particularly mentioned as present indicates that his resurrection was not merely an illusion, but a real restoration to the circumstances of daily life and friendship. It is also clear that his subsequent life after the John 11 miracle posed no small dilemma to the Jewish religious leaders. The fact that Lazarus was alive and that no one could refute the evidence that a miracle had occurred was irresistible. Because that miracle was having such an effect on the people in terms of increasing the followers of Jesus (vs. 10-11), the rulers conspired about the possibility of also putting Lazarus to death, in order to try to stop the momentum of Jesus' popularity. Albert Barnes comments: "When men are determined not to believe the gospel, there is no end to the crimes to which they are driven...Unbelief stops at no crime. Lazarus was innocent. They could bring no charge against him. But they deliberately plotted murder, rather than believe on the Lord Jesus Christ."[1]

Mary – A Loving Memorial

As the disciples and Jesus sat at supper, Mary entered the room with an alabaster box of precious ointment, worth approximately several hundred dollars in modern currency, broke the box and anointed the body of Jesus, first the head, then the feet, filling the house with the aroma (compare Mt. 26:6-13, Mr. 14:3-9, and Jno. 12:3). It was an unusual act— unexpected and unconventional, but at no point does Scripture hint of any sense of impropriety.

Jesus explained the significance to his puzzled disciples: *"Against the day of my burying hath she kept this"* (v. 7).

---

[1] *Barnes Notes on the New Testament*, p. 324.

Evidently, Mary had a keener insight to the events about to transpire than any of the other disciples. While we are told over and again that the disciples *"understood not"* (cf. 12:16) and that they either failed to remember or to properly interpret the things Jesus had said about his sufferings and death, Mary apparently took Jesus' words seriously and understood that the day was at hand. She had been saving this costly gift for just such a moment as a testimony of her love and devotion to the Savior.

What a lovely scene is this! A common woman, sacrificing what was perhaps her most precious earthly possession as an act of worship to the Savior of her soul—what could be more appropriate to the One who is God manifest in the flesh? Jesus said, *"Wheresoever this gospel shall be preached in the whole world, there shall also this, that this woman hath done, be told for a memorial of her"* (Mt. 26:13).

Judas – A Lying Thief

Judas, however, was not impressed by the display of devotion. He found no comfort in the tender expression of her love. Instead, posing as a kind of pragmatist that values social ministry above adoration and worship, Judas said, *"Why wasn't this ointment sold…and given to the poor?"* (v. 5). John adds an editorial comment to inform the reader that Judas' motives were deceptive: *"This he said, not that he cared for the poor; but because he was a thief, and had the bag, and bare what was put therein"* (v. 6). Evidently, Judas was laundering money from the treasury and disguising his covetousness in a cloak of concern for the poor.

That opportunists like Judas have used religious office for personal gain is a sad thing in the history of the cause of Christ. But we should not be surprised that there will be those who use a concern for money to cause conflict in the church and who pose to be something they are not. We may take comfort to know, however, that every Judas will eventually be exposed.

Jesus replied, *"Let her alone...for the poor ye have always with you, but me ye have not always."* There will be ample opportunity, he says, to minister to the poor. Now is a time for worship. And such an opportunity is not to be missed.

The Triumphal Entry (12:12-19)

On the day following the supper at Simon the leper's house, Jesus mounted a colt, the foal of an ass, and made his final, grand entrance into Jerusalem, a journey of approximately two miles from Bethany. All four Gospels record the Lord's triumphant entry into Jerusalem (cf. Mt. 21:1-11; Mr. 11:1-11; Lk. 19:28-40; Jno. 12:12-19). It is a strategic moment in His ministry—a public presentation and recognition of His true identity as Israel's King.

Interestingly, this event was not staged or prescripted. The only part of this event that was planned was the requisitioning of the beast that would carry the Lord Jesus. The other Gospel accounts record that Jesus sent his disciples into a neighboring village to find the animal on which he would ride. The rest of the story, including the gathering of the people along the route and their celebration of Jesus as the anticipated Messianic King was obviously a spontaneous display of adoration and worship.

When the people heard that Jesus was coming to Jerusalem they *"took branches of palm trees, and went forth to meet him, and cried, Hosanna: Blessed is the King of Israel that cometh in the name of the Lord"* (v. 13). What an amazing scene this must have been! Several lessons may be gleaned from this account.

First, we may learn something about **the humble and peaceful character of Christ's mission** in the fact that he rode, not on a stately stallion, but on a common donkey. The royal vehicle was admittedly unusual. Most dignitaries traveled by more regal means, but Jesus chose a little beast of burden, typifying his humility and meekness (cf. Zech. 9:9). The disciples used their garments as a makeshift saddle, enthroned their King on the little beast of burden, and made a triumphal carpet by placing their clothes in the path (cf. Lk. 19:35-36). Unlike any king before Him, the Lord Jesus came *"meek and lowly, riding upon a colt, the foal of an ass."* For all who feel themselves to be lowly sinners, there is comfort to be found in this One who condescended to such a low estate.

Secondly, we learn once again that **Jesus fulfilled Messianic prophecy.** *"These things understood not his disciples at the first: but when Jesus was glorified, then remembered they that these things were written of him, and that they had done these* *things unto him"* (v. 16). The prophecy in Zechariah 9 was clearly a Messianic prophecy. Though the disciples failed to make the connection at the time, they later remembered this event in light of the prophecy and, putting two and two together, understood that this act was yet another instance in which Old Testament prophecy concerning the Messiah was fulfilled in exact detail.

Thirdly, this account is yet **another proof of the Deity of Jesus Christ**. This was clearly an act of worship. The fact that Jesus did not rebuke the disciples (as the Pharisees had encouraged him to do – cf. Lk. 19:39-40), but instead accepted the homage shown Him, testifies to His deity, for only God deserves worship. In fact, Jesus indicated that if the disciples had not worshiped on this occasion, the very stones would cry out in adoration and praise.

As the people sang a portion of Psalm 118—the last of the *Hallel* Psalms sung at the annual celebration of Passover— saying, *"Blessed be the King that cometh in the name of the Lord: peace in heaven, and glory in the highest,"* they expressed worship to God for sending the Messiah who would glorify God by making reconciliation for His people. They waved "palm branches" – a symbol of victory – in their hands. It must have been a very jubilant worship service.

Finally, we may learn from this account that **legislation cannot ultimately silence the free exercise of heart religion.** *"The Pharisees therefore said among themselves, Perceive ye how ye prevail nothing? Behold, the world is gone after him"* (v. 19).

Regardless of the efforts they had made to stymie momentum, the hearts of the worshipers burst forth with praise on this occasion. How thrilling to know that that inward "well" of adoration and praise will eventually spring forth in spite of external restrictions and attempts to suppress it. What God has put in the hearts men cannot be forever restrained.

Sought by the Gentiles (12:20-36)

According to the accounts of the Triumphal Entry in Matthew and Luke, Jesus wept over Jerusalem for its unbelief as he approached the city. In that light, it is significant that John now records the fact that *"certain Greeks"* (or Gentiles) *"desired* [lit. besought or prayed] *Philip, saying 'Sir, we would see Jesus'."* (12:20-21)

This event reiterates the fact that Christ had "other sheep" that He also must bring (cf. 10:16), and that His people included Gentiles as well as Jews (cf. 3:16; 11:52). It also forecasts the fact that in just a few short years, the gospel would be sent to the Gentiles in lieu of Jewish unbelief (cf. Acts 13:46). It had been prophesied that Christ would be *"a light to lighten the Gentiles"* as well as *"the glory of his people Israel"* (cf. Is. 60:3). Now, this request by the Greeks anticipates the fulfillment of that prophecy.

When the request was communicated to Jesus, he responded, in essence, that it was not yet time to reveal Himself to the Gentiles. Something had to happen first. Gospel blessings would not be extended to the Gentiles until

193

and unless something else happened first. The *"corn of wheat"* must first die before it would *"bring forth much fruit"* (v. 24). In other words, it would only be by means of the cross that the Gentiles would be brought into gospel privilege. Hence, Jesus reiterates, in a short discourse, the importance of His death on the cross.

Christ's Death, The Model for Discipleship (vs. 23-28)

Jesus responded to the Greek's request by redirecting his disciples' attention to the urgent business at hand: *"The hour is come that the Son of man should be glorified"* (v. 23). At Cana he had said *"Mine hour is not yet come"* (2:5), and over and again throughout his public ministry we read that his hour had not yet come (cf. 7:30). Now, for the first time, he indicates that the moment for which he had entered this world had finally arrived. Obviously, he has reference to His sufferings and death on behalf of His people, or, if you please, the cross.

Next, for the benefit of his disciples, he explains, by means of an agricultural metaphor, the necessity of the cross: *"Except a corn of wheat fall into the ground and die, it abideth alone: but if it die, it bringeth forth much fruit"* (v. 24). The sentiment is clear. A seed in the grain bin, on the shelf, or in a sack will never germinate. It must be planted if it is to produce a multiple harvest. Even so, Jesus must die by means of crucifixion if a spiritual harvest is to be gained.

Then he extends the thought even further from his own death to the subject of discipleship: *"He that loveth his life shall lose it; and he that hateth his life in this world shall keep it unto life eternal. If any man serve me, let him follow me; and where I am, there shall also my servant be: if any man serve me, him will my Father honor"* (vs. 25-26). In other words, Jesus indicates that his death is the model for discipleship. Just as he would die in order to produce much fruit, so his followers should die to self and give up their lives in this world in order to gain the blessings and benefits promised to those who serve Christ.

Furthermore, Jesus models the kind of commitment to the glory of God that discipleship will entail: *"Now is my soul troubled: and what shall I say? Father, save me from this hour: but for this cause came I unto this hour. Father glorify thy name"* (vs. 27-28). If Jesus admitted the difficulty of facing his approaching death, we too can admit the inward struggles of dying to self in order to follow him. But instead of praying to be delivered from the cross, he prayed that God would be glorified in it. His concern was for the Father's glory rather than his own comfort. Such a model of self-denial is basic and fundamental to discipleship.

Christ's Death, The Means of Deliverance (vs. 29-33)

It is evident that Jesus intends to prepare his disciples for the impending trauma of his crucifixion and death. He proceeds next to emphasize that his death is necessary because it is the means of both victory over the devil and salvation for his people among the Gentiles as well as the Jews: *"Now is the judgment of this world: now shall the prince of*

195

this world be cast out. And I, if I be lifted up from the earth, will draw all men unto me. This he said, signifying what death he should die" (vs. 31-33).

By means of his death, he would destroy the devil (cf. Rev. 12:10; Heb. 2:14; 1 Jno. 3:8). The "accuser of the brethren" would be expelled from the courtroom so that he might never again condemn one of God's children (cf. Zech. 3:2; Rom. 8:33-34). Further, His people, both among the Jews and the Gentiles, i.e. *"all men,"* would be *"drawn"* to Him in covenant union.

Responding to Christ's Death: The Urgency of Discipleship (vs. 34-36)

Our Lord completes this sermon by stressing the importance of following Jesus in discipleship as the appropriate response to his death. *"Yet a little while is the light with you. Walk while ye have the light..."* (v. 35) is Jesus' way of saying that his time was short and the need was urgent. Even so today, discipleship is an urgent matter. The world grows darker by the minute. While the light of Christ through the gospel is available to us, we must follow him and so avoid the confusion of the dark world about us.

Believing & Confessing (vs. 37-50)

John concludes the record of this chapter by returning to the basic theme of his Gospel, i.e. the contrast between non-believers and believers (cf. 1:11-13).

First, he editorializes about the **unbelievers** in verses 37-41: *"But though he had done so many miracles before them, yet they believed not on him: that the saying of Isaiah the prophet might be fulfilled, which he spake, Lord who hath believed our report? And to whom hath the arm of the Lord been revealed?"* (vs. 37-38). This quotation from Isaiah 53 expressed the prophet's consternation that his message was rejected by the multitudes. Isaiah had been told at the inception of his prophetic career that his labors would have scant success (cf. Is. 6:9-13). The fact that he later bemoaned his plight, as the quotation from Isaiah 53:1 indicates, reveals just how difficult it is for God's servant to encounter rejection of the message that the Lord has given him to communicate.

Already, John's Gospel has taught us that some do not believe because they have not been born again (cf. 8:43; 10:26). Now we learn that some disbelieve because of judicial blindness: *"Therefore they could not believe, because that Isaiah said again, He hath blinded their eyes, and hardened their heart; that they should not see with their eyes, nor understand with their heart, and be converted, and I should heal them"* (vs. 39-40).

Unbelief, in its milder form (if such language is appropriate), might be defined as "doubt, or reluctance to express certainty." Such is the meaning of the term in Mark 9:24 when the father of the epileptic child said, *"Lord, I believe; help thou mine unbelief."* But when an individual becomes deeply entrenched in an attitude of hesitancy to affirm the truth, unbelief becomes a very serious sin. We might define

197

the first and most basic form of this sin by the term "reluctance," but the second, more serious form, in terms of "resistance and rebellion." This kind of unbelief that refuses to acknowledge clear and ample evidence—that rebels against the light—that resists with recalcitrance the truth of God evokes a kind of judgment from God in which the mind is blinded from truth.

Such blindness happened to Israel as a judgment from God. He had provided ample evidence that Jesus was the anticipated Messiah, but they persisted in a stubborn refusal to acknowledge the evidence; consequently, God judged the nation by blinding their eyes and hardening their hearts.

"These things said Isaiah, when he saw his glory, and spake of him" (v. 41). Though the first passage quoted from Isaiah speaks of "suffering" and the second of "glory," yet both quotations—the first from Isaiah 53 and the second from Isaiah 6—are Messianic prophecies, according to verse 41.

This is important because many of the Jews considered only the glorious side of Messianic prophecy. They took prophecies like Psalm 110:4 (*"Thou art a priest forever"*) to mean that Messiah would not die, and overlooked such passages as Isaiah 53. They could not reconcile the fact that he would reign forever with equally applicable Messianic prophecies concerning his death.

Perhaps this was the difficulty faced by the Ethiopian eunuch in Acts 8 as he read from Isaiah 53 and wondered about the identity of Jehovah's "suffering Servant." John connects the two passages, i.e. Is. 6 and Is. 53, in this verse and says they both speak of Jesus the Messiah.

Next, John reminds us that among the people of that day, there were also some who **believed but did not confess** Christ (vs. 42-43). Of course, some today would suggest that the failure to publicly acknowledge Christ is proof that their faith was spurious. But the passage gives us no such indication. We have no contextual reason to doubt the sincerity of their faith and to put them into the same category as the unbelievers of verses 37-41.

Why did this group fail to confess Christ? John answers that they feared recrimination (v. 42b). They attached too much importance to human society and personal reputation (v. 43). Obviously, this passage teaches that confession should follow belief in the Lord Jesus Christ and that God's endorsement is more to be sought than man's approval.

Finally, there are some who **believe and follow the Lord in discipleship** (vs. 44-50). To those who thus receive Him, the blessed privilege of walking in light and avoiding the darkness of error and confusion is promised.

Chapter 17
Serving One Another (John 13)

After instituting the ordinance of Communion, or the Lord's Supper, Jesus directs his focus to what this concept of "communion" means within the fellowship of the disciples.

The Example of Feet-Washing (Jno. 13:1-20)

John 13:1-20 records our Lord's lesson to his disciples at the conclusion of the Lord's Supper concerning the example of feet-washing. It is significant that this object lesson came on the heels of the first communion service. The Supper is an act of worship toward God, a vertical act of thanksgiving to God in remembrance of the Savior's atoning death. The washing of the disciples' feet is an act of service toward one another, a horizontal act of ministry to our brethren.

That the early church actually considered the washing of the saints' feet as a service Christ intended for his church to practice is clear from the requirements given for the support of bereft widows in 1 Timothy 5:10. Those who interpret the language of "washing the saints feet" as a mere euphemism for Christian service will be hard pressed to explain how the other requirements in that text for identifying "widows indeed" are also metaphorical.

Three particular lessons are communicated in this important service.

The Need for Daily Cleansing

First, feet-washing reminds believers of their ongoing need for a daily cleansing of the conscience. The language of Jesus to Peter in verses 8-10 is telling: *"He that is washed needeth not save to wash his feet, but is clean every whit."* Two separate Greek words for *"wash"* are employed in this text. He first uses the word *luou* to speak of an entire cleansing. Then he employs the word *nipto* to speak of a partial cleansing. His message, literally speaking, might be expressed like this: "He that has been washed completely does not need another entire cleansing, but just partial cleansings."

The lesson is one with which we can identify. After taking a bath at the outset of the day, a person needs merely to wash his hands before he sits down to a meal. He doesn't need another entire bath in order to sit for supper.

Obviously, Jesus intends this service to remind the disciples that they need regular, daily cleansings of conscience in the course of service to Him. Once a person has been cleansed within by the washing of regeneration (cf. Titus 3:5), he does not need a second work of grace in the soul. That work is sufficient, effectual and eternal. The regenerate child of God will never need to born again, again. His sins have been put away forever and he has been brought into an unbreakable, vital relationship with the Lord.

In terms of his fellowship with the Lord, however, he needs to confess his sins daily and appropriate, by faith, the cleansing of Christ's blood in his conscience (cf. 1 Jno. 1:7, 9). Interestingly, the word *"part"* in verse 8 derives from the Greek word *koinonia* which means "fellowship" or "communion."

The Importance of Humility

Secondly, feet-washing reminds believers of the importance of maintaining a humble attitude. There is no place for pride and self-centeredness in the life of Christian discipleship. If the Lord of glory could stoop to wash the calloused feet of fishermen and publicans, who are they to refuse to assume the same posture of self-humbling at the feet of one another?

An attitude of humility is indispensable in Christian discipleship. Over and again, the Scriptures exhort us to humble ourselves, be clothed with humility, assume the mind of Christ, and to do everything with all humbleness of mind. Humility is a way of thinking about ourselves—a mindset, if you please—in which we remember our own frailty, mortality, and depravity. This service helps us to remember those uncomfortable facts about ourselves. It's hard to be proud and arrogant when a person strikes a pose at the wrinkled feet of a brother or sister in Christ.

Churches that practice the washing of the saints' feet have a visual aid to the promotion of brotherly love. It is difficult to be at your brother's throat when you are kneeling in this menial posture at his feet. May God help every believer to maintain the servant's spirit modeled in the feet-washing service.

The Principle that We Serve the Lord by Serving Others

Finally, feet-washing reminds us that we serve the Lord by serving one another. The individual who professes to love God while neglecting to love his brother is a liar, says John (cf. 1 Jno. 4:20-21). The only way to really show our love and devotion to the Lord is by means of ministering to His little children with whom we live on a daily basis.

Indeed, the Lord's people have many flaws and blemishes and idiosyncrasies. They are not as easy to love as the One whom we have not seen. But love to our Lord may only be manifested by love to these less-than-perfect people with whom we rub shoulders each day. Jesus said, *"Inasmuch as ye have done it unto one of these the least of my children, ye have done it unto me."*

Brotherly Love (Jno. 13:21-38)

On the heels of the example of feet-washing and the intrinsic lesson that it teaches concerning the priority of serving others, our Lord reinforces the importance of brotherly love (vs. 31-35). Jesus knew that this reminder would be vital and essential to his disciples in the aftermath of his impending departure. The exhortation to love one another in verses 31-35, however, is bracketed by two counter examples to the principle of brotherly love. Jesus predicts the unloving acts both of Judas' betrayal (vs. 21-30) and of Peter's denial (vs. 36-38).

An Unloving Act of Betrayal

The Oxford English Dictionary defines the act of betrayal as "a breach of trust or a deceptive act of forfeiting a trust into the hands of an enemy by treachery." The classic Old Testament illustration of betrayal is recorded in Judges 16:18-19 when Delilah betrayed Samson's trust by revealing his secret to the Philistines. David's command to "*Set Uriah in the forefront of the hottest battle and retire from him that he may be smitten and die*" (2 Sam. 11:15) is another example of treachery, as is Absalom's ruse in the slaying of Amnon (2 Sam. 13:28). In each case, the basic dynamic of gaining someone's trust by feigning love, only to use that trust as leverage to do the unsuspecting individual harm is the essence of betrayal.

When a society becomes corrupt, incidents of betrayal are more common (cf. Micah 7:5-7). Paul writes that in the last days, men will be "truce breakers" (2 Tim. 3:3). The most intimate of relationships, he warns, will not be a safeguard against a breach of trust.

The potential to betray a trust, however, resides in every person's fallen nature. It is, in other words, an experience common to human history, and rare is the person who finishes his life as an exception to this painful experience. Even the Lord Jesus Christ would experience such pain. The Psalmist prophesies that the Messiah himself would be the victim of betrayal (cf. Ps. 41:9; 55:12-14).

Judas' betrayal of Jesus is the most diabolical act in history. By using his influence and access to Jesus as an instrument to destroy him, Judas goes down in history as the ultimate turncoat – the quintessential traitor.

An Unloving Act of Denial

Unlike Judas, Peter was a child of God. He was not an imposter. But in spite of his relationship to God, Peter still had a sinful nature and was, therefore, susceptible to fall into temptation. His denial of Jesus indicates just how powerful "peer pressure" and the desire to be accepted by the group can be. Jesus predicts that in a moment of weakness, Peter would deny his Lord on three separate occasions. Though he was not a Judas, his act of denial is nonetheless just as unloving as his colleague's betrayal.

Brotherly Love – The Badge of Discipleship

In the shadow of his death and subsequent departure from the disciples, Jesus urges upon them the priority of brotherly love as the hallmark of Christian discipleship. *"Hereby shall all men know that ye are my disciples, if ye have love one to another"* (v. 35).

The distinguishing feature of authentic Christianity is brotherly love. Is it any wonder that love is given priority among all the Christian virtues (cf. 1 Cor. 13; Gal. 5:22; Col. 3:14). Peter urged first century believers to *"see that they love one another with a pure heart fervently"* (1 Pet. 1:22). John reminded his readers that the person who says he loves God but doesn't love his brother, in deed and in truth, is a liar. Over and again, love is heralded as the greatest thing.

The early church was praised for its genuine concern for one another. "Behold how they love one another" was the report of the watching world. Even the aged apostle John, as he was dying, rallied his energies to exhort the saints, "Little children, love one another."

In a world of hatred, strife, and bitter envy, a church that truly loves the brethren is conspicuous. There is no greater advertisement to the watching world of the love of Christ to sinners than Christian love. May we who live on this side of the empty tomb never forget to *"let brotherly love continue"* (Heb. 13:1).

Chapter 18
Christ's Final Sermon (John 14-16)

John 14-16 records the last sermon delivered by Jesus prior to the crucifixion. A comparison of the timeline reveals that this message was preached even subsequent to the Olivet Discourse (cf. Mt 24; Mr. 13; Lk 21). Unlike many of his discourses, this final sermon was a message specifically directed to his disciples, not the multitudes. The theme of it is "The Ongoing Ministry of Christ to Believers through the Agency of the Holy Spirit." No single passage in the New Testament speaks more comprehensively concerning the New Covenant Ministry of the Holy Spirit than John 14-16.

Words of Comfort (vs. 1-3)

"Let not your heart be troubled..." (v. 1). Isn't it significant that the Lord Jesus, in the shadow of the cross, is more concerned about his disciples than he is for himself? Never has a more tender word fallen from the lips of man. Never has a more affecting scene presented itself. Here is the Lord of glory, preparing in a matter of mere hours to go to the cross. His words, however, are conspicuously devoid of indulgent

self-pity or personal anxiety. Instead, he speaks a word in season to the weary. His focus is on others, not himself.

It is also significant to note that Jesus did not say "Let not your life be troubled." They could not obey that imperative, for trouble is as inevitable to life as the upward motion of sparks is inevitable to fire (cf. Job 5:7). Neither the disciples then nor believers now can escape tribulation in life. In fact, *"we must through much tribulation enter into the kingdom of God"* (Acts 14:22). No, he did not say "keep trouble away from your life."

Instead he said, "Keep trouble away from your heart." Trouble is a part of life. When trouble gets inside the heart, however, the Christian is in real trouble. How important are the words of the wise man: *"Keep thy heart with all diligence, for out of it are the issues of life"* (Pro. 4:23)! By setting a sentinel at the heart's door to guard that precious fountain of all vitality and spring of life from the influx of trouble, the believer protects himself from discouragement and despair.

Here is the great challenge every Christian faces—to keep trouble from invading the heart. Once the trouble in the external world gets on the inside and gains a foothold in the believer's thought-patterns and attitudes, the enemy has virtually won the victory before the battle even starts.

But how, someone asks, can the follower of Christ keep trouble at bay from his heart? What is the prescription for calmness and quietness of soul in the midst of life's troubles?

210

Jesus answers in the next clause: *"...ye believe in God, believe also in me"* (v. 1b).

Faith in God and in the Lord Jesus Christ is the recipe for a calm heart (cf. Rom. 15:13; Is. 26:3; Phi. 4:6-8). The disciples of Jesus were in danger of losing their peace. By turning their gaze away from themselves and their own circumstances and fastening an eye of faith firmly on the Lord, they would find the inward peace and assurance necessary to proceed to the tasks at hand, even though Jesus was no longer physically present.

Our Lord proceeds to point them to five great truths that would serve to sustain their faith.

(1) **Heaven is the Father's house** – *"In my Father's house are many mansions"* (v. 2a). To say that heaven is "the Father's house" is simply to say that heaven is home. Jesus was going home—home to the Father. This home, further, is not "a little cabin in the corner of the glory world," but a home where every room is a mansion. The implication is unmistakable: all the occupants of that home (and there are many) are given royal treatment. Jesus clearly expects his followers to live with anticipation of that heavenly home where He himself was now returning.

(2) **His word is true and complete** – *"If it were not so, I would have told you"* (v. 2b). How comforting to

know that He has revealed everything we need to know and that His revelation is trustworthy! The trustworthiness and sufficiency of Scripture is a soul-cheering truth with far-reaching implications for faith and life.

(3) **Salvation is by His sovereign grace** – *"I go to prepare a place for you"* (v. 2c). We will follow him "home" some day not because of our works of preparation, but because He went to the cross to prepare a place for us. Our place in the Father's house is a gift of grace, not the result of personal merit.

(4) **Christ is coming again** – *"And if I go…I will come again and receive you to myself"* (v. 3a). There is no brighter star on the Christian horizon than the promise of the Redeemer's return. Every opponent to the kingdom of God and every obstacle to faithful discipleship will then be put away forever.

(5) **The joy of heaven will be uninterrupted fellowship with Christ** – *"That where I am, there ye may be also"* (v. 3b). To be reunited with Jesus; to see Him face to face; to know as we are known; to be like Him; to be with Him never to part again – yes, that will be glory for me.

What precious and gracious words of comfort from the lips of Jesus to His disciples! They must have drawn great comfort from these tender words then. Even today, our faith is strengthened by these great truths. Hear the word of Jesus today, my friend. *"Let not your heart be troubled."*

The Work Goes On (14:12-27)

What would happen to the work of Christ in the world once He departed? Our Lord answers that the greatest triumphs of the gospel would take place after His ascension: *"He that believeth on me, the works that I do shall he do also; and greater work than these shall he do; because I go unto my Father"* (v. 12).

Obviously Jesus does not refer to the work of eternal redemption, for that was a work that He alone could accomplish (cf. Heb. 1:3). The salvation of sinners to eternal life is a finished work (cf. Jno. 19:30). He speaks in this passage, however, of the work of the gospel church—the expansion of His cause and kingdom in this world.

When the Lord Jesus says that his followers would do "greater works" than His, he means greater in scope, not greater in importance. His influence was limited both geographically and chronologically. His three and one-half year ministry was restricted to Galilee and Judea. After His departure, however, the gospel would extend over the centuries unto the uttermost parts of the earth (cf. Acts 1:8).

The Work Proceeds by Prayer (vs. 13-15, 22-24)

Does his departure mean, then, that the Lord Jesus Christ would cease to be involved in the lives of His followers? Not at all. In His heavenly session, He would still work on behalf of His church in answer to prayer: *"And whatsoever ye shall ask in my name, that will I do, that the Father may be glorified in the Son. If ye shall ask any thing in my name, I will do it"* (vs. 13-14).

What a tremendous promise! Jesus gives His disciples the right to pray *"in [His] name."* He has granted us, in other words, "power of attorney." Believers may freely and boldly approach the Father with requests for aid not on the basis of their own right to be heard, but by virtue of the merits of Jesus in their stead. To pray "in Jesus' name" is to say, "Father, bless us, not for our own sake—not because we deserve a blessing in and of ourselves—but for thy dear Son's sake." No doubt, Fanny Crosby had this very thought in mind when she wrote the blessed line:

"Trusting only in thy merit, would I seek Thy face..."

Far from a magical spell or superstitious incantation, praying "in Jesus' name" also means asking for blessings that the Lord has already promised to give us in His word. Those who pray according to Scripture and in the spirit of the gospel pray "in His name." Believers have the right, in other words, to go to God with requests for strength, guidance, assistance, forgiveness, wisdom, understanding, and protection from evil because He has already promised us these things in His word.

Is the "power of attorney" conveyed to Christians by the Lord Jesus Christ, then, unconditional? May we use such an "authority" willy-nilly? No, again. The promise that He will continue to work in and through His followers in answer to prayer is conditional. It is made only to sincere and obedient disciples: *"If ye love me, keep my commandments"* (v. 15).

Simon the Sorcerer (in the Book of *Acts*) thought that the gift of God could be purchased for money. It could not. It is only the true and obedient Christian that is assured of Christ's ongoing ministry from heaven on his behalf.

Does this surprise you? Does it seem right that Christ's true disciples would be given benefits unavailable to others? If the conditional nature of Christ's promises seem curious to you, rest assured that you are not alone. Judas (not Iscariot), also had the same question: *"Lord, how is it that thou wilt manifest thyself unto us, and not unto the world?"* (v. 22). Our Lord responds by saying that there are blessings to be had in obedience that will not be realized in disobedience (vs. 23-24).

That eternal salvation is given to God's elect unconditionally is a great truth. Discipleship, on the contrary, is a conditional arrangement. The promise that Christ will be actuated by the prayers of those who truly love Him is not made indiscriminately. It is qualified: *"If ye love me, keep my commandments. And I will pray the Father..."* (vs. 15-16).

How then may we know if we truly "love Him"? Obedience is the proof of love: *"If a man love me, he will keep my words...He that loveth me not keepeth not my sayings"* (vs. 23a, 24a). Though God is kind to the unthankful and graciously bestows blessing on unworthy sinners, only true believers are given assurance that their prayers "in His name" will rally Heaven to their aid in the ongoing work of the gospel in this world.

The Work Proceeds by Means of the Ministry of the Holy Spirit (vs. 16-21, 25-31)

Christ's ongoing involvement from heaven in the lives of believers not only continues in response to their prayers but also by means of the New Covenant ministry of the Holy Ghost: *"And I will pray the Father and he shall give you another Comforter, that he may abide with you forever; even the Spirit of truth: whom the world cannot receive, because it seeth him not, neither knoweth him: but ye know him; for he dwelleth with you, and shall be in you. I will not leave you comfortless: I will come to you"* (vs. 16-18).

"Another Comforter" means "a second of the same kind," not "another of a different kind." The Holy Spirit, in other words, would perform precisely the same role in the lives of believers that Jesus fulfilled during his earthly life. It is only if they would lose nothing in the transition that the words of Jesus in John 16:7 – *"It is expedient for you that I go away: for if I go not away, the Comforter will not come unto you; but if I depart, I*

will send him unto you" – could be true. Were the Holy Spirit any less personally involved in the believer's life than Christ had been in the lives of his original disciples, then it would not be *"expedient,"* i.e. beneficial, for Jesus to depart.

The name "Comforter" (*parakaleo*) is rich with meaning. It refers to one who stands beside—an ally, friend, guide, advocate, strengthener, encourager, teacher, and, indeed, comforter. In his New Covenant ministry, the Holy Spirit is all of this to the church.

That the design of the Spirit's ministry is special, limited to those who believe in Jesus Christ, is emphasized in verse 17. It is only the believer who experiences the kind of intimate company and friendship that Paul terms *"the fellowship of the Spirit"* in Philippians 2:1. It is only the church that enjoys this kind of supernatural assistance and heavenly influence in its gospel endeavors. The boon and benefit of the Holy Spirit's involvement in the life of the church is vividly displayed in the *Acts of the Apostles*. Nothing accounts for the progress and longevity of the Christian church except the supernatural intervention of the risen Christ by means of the ministry of the Holy Spirit.

It is important to note that this ministry of the Spirit is subsequent to regeneration, a distinction that explains passages like Luke 11:13, where believers are promised *more* of the Spirit in answer to prayer, and Ephesians 5:18, where the verb phrase – *"Be filled with the Spirit"* – is in the passive voice yet the imperative mood, i.e. "keep on being filled."

217

This two-fold ministry of the Spirit, the first as Life-giver with eternal consequence and the second as Comforter with temporal implications, is evident when one compares John 3:3-8 and John 7:38-39. John 3 speaks of the Holy Spirit's regenerating activity ("...*born of the Spirit*") in the present tense, indicating that He was already active in that ministry. John 7, however, speaks of a ministry that the Holy Spirit would begin only after Jesus' ascension and glorification. The question begged by comparing these two passages is this: *If the Holy Spirit was already active in the work of quickening sinners, then in what sense would He be "given" after Jesus returned to heaven?*

The only way to reconcile the two passages is to understand a distinction between the Holy Spirit's ministry as it relates to the Everlasting Covenant—an arrangement that determines eternal salvation—and his role relative to the New Covenant—a covenant of worship and service. The Spirit's work as Life-giver has been going on since there was one of God's elect in this world that needed to be born again. He assumed a further role, however, at 9 a.m. Pentecost morning —a ministry to believers—as the agent of the risen Christ, to mediate His presence in the church.

It is in that sense of mediating Christ's presence in the lives of believers that verse 18 speaks: "*I will not leave you comfortless: I will come to you.*" Christ does indeed come to his followers, in the person of the Holy Spirit, so that they are not abandoned as orphans in this world. This presence of the living Christ ministered to believers by the Holy Spirit is a reality they will enjoy until resurrection morning when they will see Christ as He is and know as they are known (vs. 19-20). Ephesians 1:13-14 indicates that the Holy Spirit's ministry to those who believe is *"the earnest* [downpayment, deposit, first installment] *of our inheritance until the redemption of the purchased possession,"* that is, until resurrection day. Until then, therefore, the work of Christ will go on.

The New Covenant Ministry of the Holy Spirit (14:16-21, 25-31)

That the Holy Spirit would represent Jesus Christ as His agent to the church is the theme of John 14-16. His primary goal is "to glorify" the Son: *"He shall glorify me: for He shall receive of mine, and shall show it unto you"* (16:14). He is, as J. I. Packer expresses it, "self-effacing, directing all attention away from himself to Christ." Every other function of the Holy Spirit's ministry aims at this over-arching goal.

Teaching & Interpreting. In John 14-16, the Holy Ghost is called, no less than three times, *"the Spirit of truth."* As such, he is sent to *"teach,"* that is to make plain and interpret, *"all things"* (14:26), *"guide into all truth"* (16:13), *"testify of Christ"* (15:26), *"show things to come"* (16:13), and *"bring Christ's teaching to remembrance"* (14:26). The Holy Spirit is the Christian's resident truth teacher and it is by virtue of his ministry that we *"know the things that are freely given to us of God"* (1 Cor. 2:12-13).

219

Convicting & Convincing. Prior to his departure, Jesus made a startling statement: *"It is expedient for you that I go away"* (16:7). Then he explains the statement in terms of the Holy Spirit's cooperation with the church in her efforts to proclaim the gospel: *"And when [the Comforter] is come, he will reprove the world of sin, and of righteousness, and of judgment. Of sin, because they believe not on me. Of righteousness, because I go to my Father and ye see me no more. Of judgment, because the prince of this world is judged"* (16:8-11).

"Reprove" means "to convince." George Whitefield said it is "a conviction by way of argumentation and coming with a power upon the mind equal to a demonstration." That means that the Holy Spirit would literally prove the truth preached by gospel ministers so that it is both reasonable to the mind and real to the experience. In a word, he makes abstract truths concrete realities in the hearts and minds of the hearer.

With skill transcending the debater, the Holy Spirit argues the Divine logic of the gospel so that the hearer hears more (at least in terms of understanding) than the preacher is able to explain. With skill transcending the artist, the Holy Spirit animates words into pictures, causing hearers to experience the event as though they were actually there. He vivifies the gospel message into a "first person" narrative; he transforms a black and white picture into living color. Perhaps this what Zechariah meant when he prophesied that when God would *"pour upon them the Spirit of grace and supplications, then they would look upon Him whom they had pierced and mourn for Him as one mourneth for his only son"* (Zech. 12:10).

The preachers task would be utterly futile if this were not true. I could never convince another man of *"the exceeding sinfulness"* of his sins by the sheer art of rhetoric (cf. Rom. 7:13). I could never adequately paint the scenes of glory, or expose *"the secrets of men"* (cf. Rom. 2:14). The Holy Spirit accompanies the gospel message to convince men of their own sinfulness, of Christ's gift of righteousness, and of the enemy's defeat and judgment.

Enables & Empowers. The Holy Spirit is not only the believer's Teacher and Attorney, but also his Helper and Friend. The name Comforter conveys the thought of One who "stands beside." He works in the Christian's life as the agent of sanctification, empowering him to mortify indwelling sin and consecrate himself more and more to God in holiness. *"If ye, through the Spirit, do mortify the deeds of the body, ye shall live,"* says Romans 8:13. Note that it is the Holy Spirit that enables a believer to die to self.

It is also the Holy Spirit that sanctifies and changes the believer, more and more, into the image of Jesus Christ (cf. 2 Cor. 3:18). When Jesus speaks of this ethical transformation in Christian character, he highlights the instrumentality of the word: *"Sanctify them through thy truth; thy word is truth"* (Jno. 17:17). Of course, it is the Spirit of God that works in conjunction with God's word to enable the believer to grow spiritually.

Such growth is, of course, progressive. John 15 speaks of such progression in terms of bearing "fruit" (v. 2), "more fruit" (v. 2), and "much fruit" (v. 8). It is an important part of the Holy Spirit's ministry to assist the believer in fruit-bearing (cf. Gal. 5:22). It is in terms of his "enabling" ministry that Paul prays for the saints of Ephesus that they might be *"strengthened with might by his Spirit in the inner man."* There is reason to be encouraged with such a heavenly Helper at our side.

Abiding in Christ (Jno 15:1-8)

Our Lord continues his final message to the disciples in John 15 by discussing the need for ongoing, experiential communion and fellowship with him—a discipline expressed by the concept of *"abiding in Christ."* Though he will be no longer physically present with them, they must yet learn the moment-by-moment habit, through the Spirit, of abiding in Jesus Christ.

Jesus teaches this principle by the use of an image that would have been familiar to them,[1] i.e. a branch that draws nourishment from the vine to which it is attached: *"I am the true vine, and my Father is the husbandman"* (v. 1). The fact that the Lord calls himself the "true" vine implies that there are other supposed sources of nourishment and vitality in the world. None of the alternate means of strength and

---

[1] Palestine abounded in vineyards. Israel, itself, had been compared to a vineyard that God had planted (Is. 5:1-7; Ps. 80:8ff; Jer. 2:21).

nourishment promoted in the world, however, can make the believer productive. Jesus alone is the source of strength and sustenance to his disciples.

"Every branch in me that beareth not fruit he taketh away..." (v. 2a). The image of "fruit-bearing" conveys the idea of manifesting the effects of Christ's influence in our lives. Just because someone has been born again, however, does not automatically guarantee that he/she will produce spiritual fruit. The prepositional phrase "in me" suggests that the branch under consideration belongs to Christ in a vital relationship, but for some reason, this individual is not productive in terms of fruit-bearing in Christ's service.

Perseverance in faith and holiness, in other words, is not a decree, but a discipline. Growth in Christian character and fruitfulness in discipleship involves more than simply belonging to Christ in a vital union. The child of God who does not bear fruit is "taken away," or pruned. Though he does not lose his relationship with Christ, the fruitless person will lose the potential of fellowship with him and with his church.

Does that mean there is no discipline for the fruit-bearing believer? On the contrary: *"Every branch that beareth fruit, he purgeth it, that it may bring forth more fruit"* (v. 2b). The fruitless individual is pruned, and the fruitful individual is purged that he might be more fruitful.

The verb "to purge" means "to cleanse." One of the Heavenly Vinedresser's methods of cleansing his vineyard is by means of suffering and affliction. The Husbandman trims the excess growth, shapes the plant, and trains it to grow in a certain direction. By means of heavenly discipline, the Father, through the sanctifying ministry of the Holy Spirit, works in the lives of Christ's followers to make them more useful in Christian ministry.

God's word is the principle means of "purging" or "disciplining" believers: *"Now ye are clean through the word which I have spoken unto you"* (v. 3). When God's word is taught and proclaimed, the believer is challenged to correct his thinking and conduct so that he is once more aligned with God's revealed will. Those Christians who respond in meekness to the discipline of Scripture will have no need for the more severe discipline of being "cut off" or pruned from the fellowship of the church.

In verse four, the Lord Jesus reveals the key to maintaining a productive, fruitful Christian life: *"Abide in me, and I in you. As the branch cannot bear fruit of itself, except it abide in the vine: no more can ye, except ye abide in me."* It is important to understand that Jesus is here speaking in experiential, or existential terms. He is describing the daily, ongoing experience of remaining in close, intimate touch with the Savior.

It is the inner life of communion with and dependence on Jesus through the spiritual disciplines of prayer, meditation on holy scripture, and fellowship with other Christians that infuses strength and nourishment into the individual believer's life. It is impossible to bear fruit apart from such a close daily connection to the True Vine, the Lord Jesus Christ.

Fruit-bearing

The metaphor of fruit-bearing is simply a way of describing the dynamic of "growing in grace," or developing Christian character. In theological terms, we are talking about practical sanctification—i.e. becoming more Christ-like in terms of one's ethical conduct.

Unlike regeneration, which produces an instantaneous change in the soul, character development is progressive. Regeneration might be illustrated by the resurrection of Lazarus from death to life (cf. Jno. 11). Practical sanctification, on the other hand, is demonstrated by the healing of the blind man of Bethsaida (cf. Mr 8:22-26)—a transformation that took place in stages. Growth in grace is precisely that—growth—and growth does not happen all at once.

John 15 suggests this thought of progression when it speaks of *"fruit"* (v. 2a), *"more fruit"* (v. 2b), and *"much fruit"* (v. 8). The Lord expects his followers to grow and increase in terms of manifesting the fruit of the Spirit. Though a person has the capacity to manifest the "fruit of the Spirit" as soon as the Holy Spirit indwells the heart in regeneration, yet the Lord looks for growth both in terms of the degree and consistency of fruit produced (cf. 1 Ths. 4:1, 10b).

Producing more and more fruit in the life of discipleship involves being "filled with the Spirit" (Eph. 5:18), or, in other words, "abiding in Christ": *"I am the vine, ye are the branches: He that abideth in me, and I in him, the same bringeth forth much fruit: for without me ye can do nothing"* (Jno 15:5). If the believer allows himself to be separated from Christ in terms of daily fellowship with Him and the moment by moment habit of depending upon Jesus, he will bear no fruit.

The Christian life, in other words, is something that must be constantly sustained by means of remaining connected to the Savior. Of course, each of God's children will "abide in Christ" in terms of the vital relationship that is his by sovereign grace. John writes with certainty that *"we shall abide in Him"* (1 Jno. 2:27). Then, in the very next verse, John exhorts: *"And now, little children, abide in Him"* (1 Jno. 2:28).

How do we reconcile these two thoughts? We make sense of them both by understanding that the *union* God's child enjoys with the Savior will never cease, but *communion* may. The born again person will never lose his *relationship* with the Lord, but he may lose his *fellowship* with Him. Just as I am related to people with whom I have little to no fellowship, so a person may be one of the Father's children but enjoy no fellowship with Him. The Prodigal son was still his father's child in the hog pen, but because of his disobedience, he was cut off from the benefits of fellowship in the father's house.

The child of God may also be cut off from the source of spiritual nourishment by means of disobedience: *"If a man abide not in me, he is cast forth as a branch, and is withered; and men gather them and cast them into the fire, and they are burned"*

(v. 6). It is interesting to note the sequence in this text. It is not that he first withers and then is cast forth. Instead he is cast forth first, and then he withers. This indicates that a person may give the appearance of being a faithful Christian, although he is fruitless. The Lord knows whether or not he is really producing fruit before his companions may observe his spiritual barrenness. After the Lord prunes the fruitless professor, then the withering is manifest.

The late George Macdonald captured the sentiment of this sad dynamic: "I am deathly afraid of personal, spiritual deterioration. A man may sink by such slow degrees that long after he is a devil, he may still give the appearance of being a good churchman, theologian, or Christian." I, too, am afraid of such a slow deterioration of my spiritual vigor and zeal, imperceptible to the public but seen by the Lord, and every Christian should be too. Let us not be found in the condition of the church at Sardis, having a reputation that we are alive while all the while we are dead.

How can one prevent such a personal tragedy in his/her spiritual life? By staying connected to the Lord Jesus Christ through the spiritual disciplines of prayer, bible study, meditation, and fellowship with the saints: "*If ye abide in me and my words abide in you, ye shall ask what ye will and it shall be done unto you*" (v. 7). The necessity of staying in the word in order to maintain one's spiritual strength and daily focus cannot be overstated.

227

Why should we be concerned to bear fruit in Christ's service? Because it is by this means that God is glorified: *"Herein is my Father glorified, that ye bear much fruit; so shall ye be my disciples"* (v. 8). An authentic Christian is not someone who simply professes to believe in Jesus, but one who abides in Him and bears fruit.

The exhortation to abide in Christ involves both allowing His word to abide in us (v. 7; cf. Col. 16) and abiding in His love: *"As the Father hath loved me, so have I loved you: continue ye in my love"* (15:9). Jesus expects his followers to manifest the same love to Him and to one another that the Father manifested to the Son, and the Son to the disciples.

To *"continue"* (or *abide, dwell, remain*) in His love means to carry on that legacy of love in this loveless world. First, Christians must continue to love Him. This is the thought in the next verse: *"If ye keep my commandments, ye shall abide in my love,"* that is to say, "in love to me" (v. 10). The Lord Jesus expects his disciples to maintain a burning devotion to him. How is such love to Christ displayed? It is manifested by obedience to His commandments (cf. 14:23).

Love to the Savior is not simply a matter of rendering lip-service. *"Let us not love in word or tongue,"* says John, *"but in deed and truth"* (1 Jno. 3:18). The best proof of love to Christ is an obedient submission to His word (cf. 1 Jno. 5:2).

Love to Christ comes first. The believer who is devoted to the Lord and manifests that devotion by a commitment to obey His word will experience the joy of love, such as Jesus exhibited during his earthly life and ministry: "*These things have I spoken unto you, that my joy might remain in you, and that your joy might be full*" (v. 11). The joy of this love relationship with Christ is inexpressibly sweet. It is pictured in the *Song of Solomon* in the most romantic terms. It was also the impetus of so many Christian hymns composed in centuries past. Indeed, there is no joy like the joy of love. Neither the joy of victory, nor the joy of a task accomplished can match the joy of love.

Abiding in Christ's love, however, does not only involve continuing in love to Him. It also involves continuing in brotherly love: "*This is my commandment, That ye love one another, as I have loved you*" (15:12). The closer one lives in loving fellowship with Christ, the more spontaneous his heart will spring forth and overflow in love to other believers.

This "*commandment*" to love fellow believers is the royal law of Christianity (cf. Rom. 13:8-10). The person who loves his brother has fulfilled the law of Christ, for love will never do anything to the harm or detriment of another. Love seeks the loved one's best interest and welfare, both physically and spiritually.

What is the model for love to fellow believers? It is Christ's own love to us: "*...as I have loved you*" (v. 12). The Christian who seeks to continue the legacy of Christ's love must take his cue from the Lord Jesus and model his love after the Savior's.

Then, what kind of love did Jesus manifest to his disciples? It was *a self-sacrificing love*: "*Greater love hath no man than this, that a man lay down his life for his friends"* (15:13). Love that dies to self-interest for the benefit of another is truly the highest expression of love. How contrary is such an idea to our world of self-protection, self-fulfillment, and self-gratification. The greatest love of all is not a matter of learning to love oneself, but a matter of dying to self to make the loved one great. When we too practice such sacrificial concern for others above ourselves, we show ourselves to be the friends of Jesus (v. 14).

The love of Christ to His disciples was also a **transparent, and accessible love**: *"Henceforth I call you not servants; for the servant knoweth not what his lord doeth: but I have called you friends; for all things that I have heard of my Father I have made known unto you"* (15:15). Jesus withheld or concealed nothing from his disciples that was profitable to them. He kept no secrets but communicated openly and freely with them.

If we will continue in his love, we must also be committed to sharing in common with other Christians the things that God has taught and given us. Love does not hide and hoard in miserly, self-concern. It lives with an open hand and an open heart, "ready to distribute, willing to communicate."

This manifestation of love to Christ and his people is the kind of fruit that followers of the Lord Jesus have been commissioned to produce (v. 16). This is what it means to be a Christian. This is the very reason he chose his disciples and sent them into the world—to carry on the legacy of His love.

May every Christian abide in Christ, by obeying his command to "love one another" (v. 17).

Expect Persecution (15:18 – 16:4)

After discussing the promise of the Spirit (ch. 14), and the principle of fruit-bearing by means of abiding in Christ (ch. 15), Jesus addresses the third and final major point in this, his farewell address to the disciples, i.e. an exhortation to expect opposition from the world (ch. 15:18 – 16:4). He does not want the disciples to approach ministry with unrealistic expectations or to be alarmed by the ill treatment they will receive from this fallen world system.

The Lord Jesus was a realist. He expected his disciples, consequently, to maintain realistic expectations of the kind of treatment they would receive from the world. He intended to protect them from cherishing any illusions about their own popularity. He didn't want them to be surprised when they encountered rejection of their message, personal recrimination, privation, or hardship because of their commitment to Jesus Christ. He warned them in advance lest they should become discouraged when the public at large showed little interest in their proclamation of the gospel message.

Why, someone may wonder, did the Lord wait until the very end of his earthly life and ministry to divulge such a harsh reality to his disciples? Jesus had not gone into this amount of detail earlier because he was still present with them; however, now that he was leaving them, he knows that full disclosure of the kind of reaction they can expect from the world is important (16:4).

Notice the reasons that the followers of Jesus must anticipate foul treatment from the world. First, they can expect rejection simply **by virtue of their identification with Jesus Christ**: *"If the world hate you, ye know that it hated me before it hated you. If ye were of the world, the world would love his own: but because ye are not of the world, but I have chosen you out of the world, therefore the world hateth you"* (15:18-19).

He proceeds to remind them that *"The servant is not greater than his lord. If they have persecuted me, they will also persecute you..."* (v. 20) and that *"...all these things will they do unto you for my name's sake"* (v. 21a). Jesus was never widely accepted by this world. Likewise, his true followers will always be in the minority. The individual who aligns himself with Jesus, should not expect any better treatment from this fallen world than the Master himself received.

'Why,' perhaps you ask, 'is the general public so antagonistic to Christianity'? Our Lord answers in verse 21b: *"...because they know not him that sent me"* (cf. 16:3). Those who persecute the followers of Christ are motivated by a radical ignorance of the true God that distorts their entire perspective.

Theologians categorize this deep-seated, heart ignorance as one of the *noetic effects of sin* — a description of how indwelling sin distorts & disfigures the natural man's entire perception of

232

life and the world. This skewed perspective of the natural man is, as Ephesians 4:18 defines it, a "heart ignorance," i.e. a visceral animosity that clouds a person's rational judgment: *"Having the understanding darkened, being alienated from the life of God through the ignorance that is in them, because of the blindness of their heart."*

Notice that Paul explains his pre-Damascus Road activities of persecuting Christians in terms of this native "heart ignorance" (cf. 1 Tim. 1:13). Likewise, he explains the motives of those who crucified the Lord of Glory in terms of this same malady (cf. 1 Cor. 2:8). Did not our Lord himself highlight this dynamic of "heart ignorance" when he prayed on the cross, *"Father forgive them, for they know not what they do"* (Lk. 23:34).

This distorted perspective resident in the natural mind is an ignorance born from a deep, emotional antipathy (not only toward the Son but also toward the Father – cf. 15:23), and the only remedy for it is regeneration. Mere education is not adequate. It takes a radical change wrought by the Holy Spirit in the soul, such as Paul experienced on Damascus Road (Acts 9).

Secondly, the disciples of Jesus Christ can expect persecution **because their message is confrontational**: *"If I had not come and spoken to them, they had not had sin: but now they have no cloak for their sin"* (15:22). The message Jesus proclaimed did not coddle the crowd. He did not play to the popular palate. He spoke truth without catering to the crowd. His words exposed the hypocrisy of the scribes and Pharisees.

The Lord called sinners to repentance and warned the disobedient of Divine judgment. He condemned human exploitation and class envy. He crossed the societal boundaries of racial prejudice and completely dismissed their faulty preconceptions of social and ethnic superiority. Those of us who seek to continue the process of promoting that same message may expect comparable opposition.

Third, the miracles of Jesus put him in a different classification from everyone else and *the ungodly world feels the need to destroy whatever is different and unique*: *"If I had not done among them the works which none other man did, they had not had sin: but now have they both seen and hated both me and my Father"* (15:24). You can see this very dynamic in popular culture today. Anyone who is different and wholesome is fair game. This sinful world feels compelled to destroy the person who exhibits integrity, wisdom, non-conformity to its standards, and disinterest in its approval.

The bottom line of these warnings is clear. Jesus does not want his followers to think that they are exceptions to the rule (cf. 16:1). They must not expect accolades and kudos from this world. They must not be ambitious for popularity. In fact, the person who seeks great things for himself, like fame or fortune, better count the cost before putting his hand to the plow of Christian discipleship, for persecution is every Christian's lot (cf. 1 Tim. 3:12).

With this hard-hitting example of full disclosure, the promise of the Holy Spirit's heavenly assistance to believers is

234

even more reassuring and comforting (15:26-27). How crucial is this warning to Christians today! How salutary is this reminder to every professed believer who thinks he can have the best of both worlds! God help us to maintain realistic expectations in Christian service.

Summary (16:5-33)

The Lord concludes his message to the disciples as he began it, i.e. seeking to encourage them in their sorrow. The passage recorded in John 16:5-33 builds on the contrast between two key words—"*sorrow*" and "*joy*." Jesus knows that his faithful followers would experience deep sorrow, both at the point of separation from him and subsequently when they meet with rejection and opposition from this unbelieving world (cf. 16:6). It would be unrealistic and unhealthy to deny that fact. At the same time, he outlines four great truths to temper and mitigate their sorrow.

(1) The Ministry of the Holy Spirit (vs. 7-15). Though they were sorrowful, yet, Jesus insists, it was "*expedient*" (the Greek word means "profitable" or "advantageous") for him to depart, else the Comforter would not come (v. 7). The only way that they would be benefited by Jesus' departure is if the Holy Spirit would fulfill at least an equal and identical role toward them that Jesus had filled during his physical presence.

How would the Holy Spirit assist them in their task of ministry? He would accompany the message they preached to *"reprove"* (or "convince and convict") the world of sin, righteousness, and judgment (v. 8). In particular terms, the Holy Spirit would attend the preaching of the word, convicting hearers, in the process, of the sin of unbelief (v. 9). This very thing happened when Peter preached at Pentecost and called his Jewish hearers to repent of the sin of crucifying their Messiah. Three thousand were *"pricked in their hearts,"* convicted of the sin of unbelief, and brought to respond to the message in repentance and faith (Acts 2:38-42).

The Spirit of God will also convince hearers concerning the gift of Christ's imputed righteousness—a fact proved by the resurrection (v. 10; cf. Rom. 4:25). When the disciples preach about the finished work of Jesus Christ, the Holy Spirit validates that truth in the hearts of believing hearers. Thirdly, the Holy Spirit assists Jesus' disciples when they proclaim the sentence of Divine judgment that has been passed upon the devil (v. 11; cf. Jno. 12:31-32).

In a word, the gospel preaching of those who would seek to represent Christ in subsequent ages would be empowered by the unction of the Holy Spirit attending the message (cf. 1 Pet 1:12; 1 Ths 1:5; 1 Cor 2:4). The Spirit's accompaniment of gospel preaching would take the form of a demonstration (the verb "to show" in vs. 13-15 literally means "to demonstrate"). The promise that the Holy Spirit would accompany the gospel proclaimed by Jesus' followers is the first reason cited to assuage their sorrow and give them joy.

(2) The Promise of His Return (vs. 16-22). The second antidote to their sorrow is the promise of the Savior's glorious return. Jesus illustrates this principle with the familiar image of a woman's sorrow during labor—a sorrow that is largely forgotten when the joyful arrival of a newborn child is realized. Even so, all of our sorrows will be over when the Savior returns (cf. Rom. 8:18). The anticipation of that happy day, in the meantime, is a source of great joy to believers.

(3) The Promise of Personal Communion with the Father through Prayer (vs. 23-27). Thirdly, Jesus cites the privilege of approaching God in prayer as an antidote to sorrow and a means of joy: *"Hitherto have ye asked nothing in my name: ask, and ye shall receive, that your joy may be full"* (v. 24).

There is great joy to be found in answered prayer. The best antidote for a sorrowful heart is to pour out your complaints before the Father in prayer. Ask for his help and grace. The joy to be found in communion with God is tremendous.

(4) The Knowledge that Christ has Overcome the World (v. 28-33). Finally, Jesus indicates that the knowledge that he has overcome the world should make us *"of good cheer."* The world's temptations and pitfalls did not defeat our Lord. He lived a victorious life. So, too, may we, by faith in him (cf. 1 Jno. 5:4).

This final sermon from our Lord's ministry begins with the sweetness of heavenly comfort—*"Let not your heart be troubled"*—and ends with the assurance of heavenly peace —*"In me you might have peace...I have overcome the world."* In

237

the body of the message, Jesus speaks precious promises (Jno. 14), reveals God's program for discipleship (Jno. 15), and warns of persecution from the world (Jno. 16). A lifetime of study and meditation will not exhaust the riches contained in it. Truly, never man spake like the Lord Jesus.

Chapter 19
Jesus Prays for His Own (John 17)

Affter preaching to his disciples (Jno 14-16), Jesus then prayed for them (Jno 17). This prayer is a kind of "preview of coming attractions"—an object lesson of the Savior's heavenly session on behalf of his people. It is as if our Lord is answering the question in advance, "You wonder what I will be doing on your behalf and in your interest after I have gone away? I will be making intercession for you in a manner not unlike this prayer."

No commentary on this audible prayer made in the interest of his disciples and prayed in their presence can possibly exhaust its rich meaning. One has the sense that he is eavesdropping on the Holy of Holies as he reads this rich passage. We are truly standing on holy ground in John 17.

Don't hurry through this prayer. It is too substantive for a simple cursory glance. It demands close inspection and reflection. And it deserves a humble and heartfelt response of adoration.

The Significance of this Prayer

John 17 is a prayer of praise, thanksgiving and petition, but most of all, it is a prayer of intercession. As such, this chapter

239

telegraphs the kind of ongoing ministry in which Christ our great High Priest is engaged on behalf of his people in his post-resurrection session in heaven.

The priesthood of Jesus Christ is a glorious doctrine. It is one of the dominant themes of the book of *Hebrews*. It is also the theological basis implicit in John 17.

The writer of *Hebrews* highlights two primary aspects of Christ's priesthood: 1) the Priest's *person*, and 2) His priestly *work*.

First, in terms of the *person* of our great High Priest, Hebrews informs us that 1) He is divinely *called*, as was Aaron (Heb. 5:4-6), having been chosen by the Father in covenant to occupy this role; 2) He is *compassionate* to both the ignorant and wayward (Heb. 5:1) and the suffering and afflicted (Heb. 4:14-16; 2:17-18); 3) He is *changeless*, unlike earthly priests who died and faded from usefulness (Heb. 7:23-27).

Next, in terms of our Priest's *work*, the Lord Jesus represents his people before the Father in both priestly functions—offering sacrifice for sin (Heb. 8:3) and making intercession (Heb. 7:25). This dual function compares to the role filled by the Old Testament, Levitical priest as he represented the covenant people before Jehovah.

Unlike the priests under the Law, however, our great High Priest did not offer animal sacrifices, which could never take away sin. Instead, he offered himself, fulfilling both the role of Priest and Lamb simultaneously: *"...but now once in the end of the world hath he appeared to put away sin by the sacrifice of himself...So Christ was once offered to bear the sins of many..."* (Heb. 9:26b, 28a). And unlike the Levites whose work was repetitive and unceasing, Christ our Priest made one offering of perpetual, atoning efficacy: *"And every priest standeth daily ministering and offering oftentimes the same sacrifices which can never take away sins: but this man, after he had offered one sacrifice for sins for ever, sat down on the right hand of God...for by one offering he hath perfected forever them that are sanctified"* (Heb. 10:11-12, 14).

Do we wonder to whom Jesus our Priest offered himself as a sacrifice? He did not offer himself to the devil. Nor did he offer himself to the sinner. He *"offered himself without spot to God"* (Heb. 9:14). And God accepted that "once for all time" offering. It achieved its objective (cf. Heb. 10:11).

Christ's priestly work did not end, however, with his sacrifice on the cross. He did not retire from the priesthood after Calvary, but arose from the grave three days later to begin his intercessory ministry. Even to this present hour, the one who *"made reconciliation for the sins of the people"* is still our *"merciful and faithful high priest, able to succor them that are tempted"* who *"ever lives to make intercession for us"* (Heb. 2:17-18; 7:25).

What are the implications of this truth to us today? It means that Jesus still prays for his people—that he is now doing in heaven the very thing he did for his disciples in John 17. In terms of his atoning and redemptive sacrifice, Christ's intercession and presence at the Father's right hand is our guarantee of final salvation (cf. Rom. 8:34; 5:10). He rose from the dead to insure that all for whom he died will receive the benefits of his atoning death. The Testator that died now lives as the Executor of his own vast estate, of which estate we are heirs by virtue of God's electing grace.

In temporal terms, Jesus lives and ministers as our great High Priest in heaven in order to purge the conscience of penitent sinners from daily guilt (cf. Heb. 9:14; 1 Jno. 2:1-2) and to spread the burdens and cares of his church before the Father via intercessory prayer (cf. Lk. 22:32; Heb. 10:19-22; Rom. 8:27).

What would it mean to you to know that the President's own son was lobbying for you in the Oval Office? Would you not be confident that your case would be heard with the utmost concern and compassion? Likewise, to know that the Father's own Son is our Advocate before the heavenly throne, ready to stand up to plead for us when we are in need, just as he stood up in defense of his faithful martyr Stephen builds great confidence and boldness in our hearts. Such is the significance of this prayer in John 17.

The General Content of this Prayer

In John 17, then, we see our great High Priest at work. It is an acted sermon, answering the question that must have been in the minds of his disciples, "What will you do when you are no longer with us?" John 17 replies, "I will be praying for you when I have gone home to the Father." Do we wonder what

Christ our Priest says in his intercessory role before the throne of God? Again, John 17 is our object lesson.

The Lord Jesus emphasizes three great themes in this high-priestly prayer. First, he prayers concerning the **salvation** of his people (vs. 1-5). Secondly, he prays concerning the **sanctification** of his disciples (vs. 6-21). Finally, he prays concerning the **glorification** of all that were given to him by the Father (vs. 22-24).

Further, our Lord prays for three groups of people in John 17. First, he prays for *"those given to him by the Father"* (v. 2). Next, he prays for *"the men which Thou gavest me out of the world"* (v. 6), i.e. Peter, James, John, Andrew, Matthew, etc. Thirdly, Jesus prays for all believers—*"them that shall believe on me through their word"* (v. 20), i.e. you, me and all in subsequent ages who would come to gospel faith by means of the apostolic testimony in Scripture.

We might also analyze the prayer in terms of the three "gifts" referenced by our Lord: (1) The gift of eternal life (*"...that he should give eternal life to as many as thou hast given him"* - v. 2); (2) The gift of God's word (*"I have given unto them the words which thou gavest me..."* - v. 8); (3) The gift of glory (*"And the glory which thou gavest me I have given them..."* - v. 22).

Yet again, the Savior's prayer emphasizes three time-zones: the past, i.e. *"before the world was"* (vs. 1-5), the present, i.e. *"in the world"* (vs. 6-21), and the future, or the eternal state (v. 24).

Finally, we might examine the prayer by considering Jesus' emphasis on the word "glory." First, he is concerned to

243

"glorify" the Father in the work of salvation (v. 1). Next, he prays for the work of the church that the Son would be "glorified in them" [i.e. in his followers or disciples] (v. 10). Then, he emphasizes the glorification of all the elect in the last day (vs. 22-24).

Let's put these various analyses together. In verses 1-5, Jesus intercedes for all the elect in the interest of their need for eternal life. The focus here is one people who were given to the Son in the everlasting covenant and whose salvation would be secured upon the cross, by which event the Son would glorify the Father. In verses 6-21, Jesus intercedes for the church, i.e. the original disciples and all believers in subsequent ages, or those described in vs 11 and 14 as "*in but not of the world*," that they might be kept safe in the world, sanctified by the word, and glorify their Lord by going "*into the world*" (v. 18) so that "*the world may believe*" (v. 21b), i.e. to make disciples of all nations. The focus here is on the present needs and challenges the church of the Lord Jesus Christ faces in a world that is antagonistic to the truth of God. Finally, in verses 22-24, Jesus again intercedes for his entire family, that they may, in the future, eternal state, be glorified and be with him forever in heavenly bliss.

However we analyze this solemn and cheering prayer, it is evident that our Lord in his intercessory ministry is concerned not only about the eternal salvation of the elect family of God, but also about the temporal welfare and ministry of his disciples in this world. In fact, the bulk of the prayer, verses 6-

21, focuses on the protection of believers and the prosperity of the gospel in this world.

There is one final observation, in terms of this general overview of the Savior's prayer, we might make. This prayer suggests six characteristics of Christ's disciples that we see manifested in the history of the early church in Acts.

For example, Jesus prays that his disciples would experience his "joy" in themselves (v. 13). Is it any wonder that at least twenty times in the *Acts of the Apostles* we read about the joy of Jesus' disciples (cf. Acts 2:46; 8:8).

Secondly, Jesus prays that his disciples would be kept "safe" in the world (v. 11). The story of Peter's deliverance from prison in Acts 12 and of Paul's rescue from shipwreck in Acts 27 are examples of the way God answers this prayer.

Thirdly, Jesus prays for the "sanctification" of believers through the word (v. 17). Acts 6:7 gives us an example of how the word of God was blessed to consecrate believers to a life of obedient devotion to God.

Fourth, Jesus prays for the "evangelistic success" (vs. 18, 20). Acts 8:4 describes how the gospel spread beyond its initial circle to encompass all nations.

Fifthly, the Lord Jesus prays concerning the "unity" of his church (v. 21). Acts 2:46 and 4:32 present a beautiful picture of the brethren dwelling together in the unity of the faith.

Finally, Jesus prays that his "love" may be manifest in his church (v. 26). This kind of brotherly love was a dominant mark of the early church, as Barnabas himself personifies in Acts 9:27.

Our Lord is still praying on behalf of his church in this world concerning these key virtues. He still intercedes on our behalf that we might experience joy, safety, holiness, gospel converts, gospel unity, and brotherly love. Are we not thankful that he is interested in us at a level even beyond our final happiness?

The Specific Details of this Prayer
The Gift of Eternal Life: Salvation (vs. 1-5)

As stated, Jesus prays first in this momentous prayer concerning the eternal salvation of his people (vs. 1-5). He begins by saying, *"Father, the hour is come; glorify thy Son, that thy Son also may glorify thee"* (v. 1).

Throughout his public ministry, Jesus spoke of "his hour." When his mother urged him to demonstrate his Divine identity by performing a miracle at the wedding feast in Cana, Jesus replied, *"Mine hour is not yet come"* (Jno. 2:4). Later, when his brothers prodded him to announce his Deity, he again responded, *"My time is not yet come"* (Jno. 7:6). Further, John explains that initial efforts by the Jewish religious leaders to apprehend him were thwarted because *"his hour was not yet come"* (Jno. 8:20). As he neared the cross, however, our Lord acknowledged, *"The hour is come, that the Son of man should be glorified"* (Jno. 12:23). It is clear that the Lord Jesus lived with a perpetual sense of God's timing, interpreting all of life in terms of this "hour," the moment for which he had come into the world. That moment of ultimate, strategic importance—the defining moment of redemptive history—has now arrived.

Verse one also highlights the great aim, or goal, of the work of Christ, i.e. the glory of God in the salvation of sinners: "...Glorify thy Son, that thy Son also may glorify thee." The petition "glorify thy Son" is a request for the Father to honor the Son in his sacrificial work by accepting the offering he makes for sin. And in accepting the work of the Son on the cross, the Father would be glorified, in all subsequent ages.

It is significant that as he approaches the cross, the Savior's greatest desire is the glory of his Father, not his own personal comfort. Although Jesus went to Calvary because people needed salvation, his primary goal was the glory of God. Here is the great aim of redemption—the glory of God.

It has been said that God does all things either for man's good or for his glory. But Scripture teaches that even those things that he does for our good aim ultimately at his greater glory. Do you wonder why Jesus went to the cross? Was it because his people needed salvation from sin? Yes, indeed. The cross was critical to our good. But the primary reason the Lord of glory humbled himself to suffer and die was the Father's glory.

Ephesians 1 indicates that in Christ, God has given to human beings every necessary spiritual blessing—election, predestination, adoption, justification, sanctification, redemption, and forgiveness. Did we need these blessings? Absolutely! Notice, however, a thrice-repeated phrase that indicates the ultimate motive and aim of these bestowed mercies: *"To the praise of the glory of His grace"* (Eph. 1:6, 12, 14). The glory of God in the salvation of sinners was the Savior's primary objective as he went to the cross. In an age of such excessive subjectivity as ours, we need to take special notice of this truth.

Was the Father glorified by means of Christ's work at the cross? Yes, and he is still receiving glory for it today. We sing about it, meditate upon it, preach about it, talk about it with other believers, and praise him for it still, these twenty-odd centuries after the fact. Thousands upon thousands have sought to express their gratitude for such an unspeakable gift by giving their lives in the service of this God who, through his dear Son, demonstrated his faithful love. In fact, eternity will be filled with anthems of praise to the God whose wisdom solved man's greatest problem, whose power conquered man's greatest foe, and whose grace met man's greatest need. Jesus saw the cross as an opportunity to promote the glory of God for the ages to come.

"As thou hast given him power over all flesh, that he should give eternal life to as many as thou hast given him" (17:2). In verse 2, our Lord affirms both his universal sovereignty and his particular grace. As one of the provisions of the everlasting covenant, the Father conferred upon the Son (who had voluntarily assumed the office of Mediator) sovereign

authority over all mankind. Jesus Christ is, indeed, the sovereign King of the universe. But though his sovereign sway extends to every man, woman, boy and girl that has lived, lives now or will live in the future, his grace is definite and particular in its scope. He gives the gift of eternal life to "as many as" the Father gave him, that is, to the elect.

These words, and many like them in Scripture, form the basis of the great doctrine of *definite atonement*, or *particular redemption*. Jesus Christ did not die for all men indiscriminately, but for a special, particular, and limited number of the human family. The Bible says that he gave his life for "his people" (cf. Is. 53:8; Ps. 111:9; Mt. 1:21), the "sheep" (Jno. 10:11, 15), and those "sanctified" (lit. distinguished) and given to him in covenant before the world began (cf. Heb. 10:14; Jno. 6:37; Eph. 1:4). Eternal life is given to those *"for whom it is prepared of the Father"* (Mt. 20:23).

Notice further, as verse 2 affirms, that eternal life is a *gift*. The Lord Jesus Christ **gives** it*"to as many as the Father gave him."* Salvation from sin is a gift bestowed, not a wage or reward earned. Ephesians 2:8 concurs: *"For by grace are ye saved through faith; and that not of yourselves: it is the gift of God: not of works, lest any man should boast."*

People neither earn nor deserve salvation from their sins. Instead, God, without obligation or coercion, takes the initiative to meet the need of persons that cannot help themselves, and to favor people who deserve the very opposite of that kindness.

249

"And this is life eternal that they might know thee the only true God, and Jesus Christ, whom thou hast sent" (17:3). Verse 3 indicates that the "eternal life" that Jesus graciously gives to his people consists of a relationship with the Father and the Son.

Eternal life, in other words, is not simply a synonym for the *immortality of the soul*. Indeed, the Bible teaches immortality, i.e. that human beings consciously survive death and continue forever (cf. Ecc. 3:21; Gen. 35:18; 1 Kings 17:21-22; Rev. 6:9). The soul lives on after physical death in one of two places, either heaven (cf. Lk. 23:43; Acts 7:59; 2 Cor. 5:8; Mt. 17:3) or hell (cf. Lk. 16:23-31; Mt. 10:28). Death is not annihilation; it does not equate to cessation of existence.

A popular syllogism employed in classical apologetic circles makes a case for immortality (and against annihilationism) from the premise of the existence of God.[1] The *a priori* argument is as follows:

1. The self-existent God created man in his image, as a personal, rational and
   moral being.
2. A personal God would not annihilate that which is like himself in these essential ways.
3. Therefore, human beings are immortal.

---

[1] Norman Geisler, *Baker Encyclopedia of Christian Apologetics*, p. 354.

Likewise, a rational case can be made for immortality (and against annihilationism) from the moral premise of the justice of God.[2] The argument from ultimate justice goes like this:

1. A righteous God is the ultimate standard of justice.
2. Ultimate justice is not always achieved in this life.
3. Therefore, another life in which ultimate justice is achieved must exist.

A very compelling argument for immortality, in my opinion, derives from the universal principle of existential longing in human nature, a principle spelled out in Ecclesiastes 3:11: *"He hath made every thing beautiful in his time: also **he hath set the world in their heart,** so that no man can find out the work that God maketh from the beginning to the end"* [emphasis mine]. This verse describes a familiar dynamic—the yearning to know, understand and experience the full spectrum of the cosmos in all of its beauty, and yet the frustration in human experience arising from the inability to achieve that objective. The verse further traces this existential yearning and desire to discover ultimate meaning to the fact that God has put *"the world"* (lit. eternity) in the human heart.

Taking his cue from this principle of human longing, the Oxford intellectual C. S. Lewis codified a popular argument for immortality as follows:[3]

---

[2] Ibid. p. 355
[3] Ibid.

1. Every innate desire and longing has a real object capable of fulfilling it.
2. Human beings have an instinctive desire and longing for immortality.
3. Therefore, there must be an immortal life after death.

In his *Handbook of Christian Apologetics*, Peter Kreeft develops Lewis' premise in practical terms. He says that just as the experience of hunger and thirst presupposes the reality of food and drink, and the desire for knowledge presupposes the reality of objective truth, so the subjective longing for paradise, heaven or eternity presupposes that every human being is immortal.[4]

That the concept of "eternal life" for which Jesus prays in John 17 is something distinct from immortality, however, is evident by the fact that he defines it in relational terms: *"This is life eternal that they might know thee the only true God, and Jesus Christ, whom thou hast sent."* Of course, even the wicked will experience immortality, albeit in hell. But eternal life is exclusive to those whom the Father gave to the Son in the everlasting covenant: *"...that he should give eternal life to as many as thou hast given him."*

So, eternal life does not merely mean that someone will live forever. It involves something more than a sheer perpetual existence. This is clear from Jesus' use of the verb "to know" in verse 3. As is frequently the case in Scripture, "to know" is

---

[4]Ibid. p. 355.

a relational term. It speaks of a covenant relationship and the attending intimacy and familiarity of relational love (cf. Amos 3:2; Mt. 7:23; Gen. 4:1). From the Savior's words in verse 3 then, we may legitimately define eternal life as "a perpetual existence characterized by relational union and communion with the Father and the Son." It is, in other words, more of a qualitative than a quantitative dynamic.

This heavenly quality of life consists of an ever-deepening knowledge of the true and living God. The heaven that awaits God's elect, in other words, will never foster an attitude of boredom or apathy, but ever-increasing delight and satisfaction in communion with God. We will never cease to be enthralled by his glory. Heaven will not be like so many marriages, where one partner learns the other through and through, then slips into a spirit of complacency and boredom. Familiarity with God will not breed a spirit of monotony, but continual and growing fascination with his Divine charms. Knowing God and growing ever deeper in our relationship with him, is the chief business of heaven.

Further, this sublime, never-ending relationship with God that the Bible calls "eternal life" is a gift of God's free and sovereign grace. By what means would the Lord Jesus give the gift of eternal life to his covenant people? Verse 4 answers in terms of the finished work of Christ at the cross: *"I have glorified thee on the earth: I have finished the work which thou gavest me to do."*

Of course, Jesus had not yet gone to the cross when he prayed this prayer. In what sense then, someone wonders, does he speak in the past tense as if the covenant assignment conferred upon him by the Father had already been finished? Scripture answers unequivocally: God considered the salvation of his elect guaranteed, even before the actual redemptive transaction occurred, by virtue of his own covenant faithfulness. Jesus' words must be interpreted, in other words, as covenantal language.

This covenantal paradigm is the basis for interpreting Paul's argument in Romans 3:24-25: *"Being justified freely by his grace through the redemption that is in Christ Jesus: whom God hath set forth to be a propitiation through faith in his blood, to declare his righteousness for the remission of sins that are past, through the forbearance of God..."* In this passage, Paul answers the question, "On what basis can God be just to forgive the sins of people that lived prior to the cross?" Paul responds, "He was just to do so because of his covenant faithfulness."

Christ was "set forth" or foreordained, he says, as the One who would satisfy the justice and wrath of God. When was he thus foreordained? Obviously, in the intra-Trinitarian council of eternity past. This is clearly a reference to the everlasting covenant before the world began, a unilateral compact between the Father, the Son and the Holy Spirit in which the Second Divine Person voluntarily agreed to be the sin-bearer (cf. 2 Tim. 1:9; Heb. 13:20; Eph. 1:4; 1 Cor. 2:7; Jno. 6:37-39; Is. 6:8; 48:16; 2 Sam. 23:5). That covenant was grounded on the faithfulness of the God who cannot lie (cf. Titus 1:2; Heb. 6:16-20; 2 Tim. 2:13; Rom. 3:3; 11:26-29). As the covenant-keeping God looked forward in faithful anticipation to the actual payment of the redemptive price he had pledged in covenant, therefore, he was justified to remit the sin-debt of his covenant people who lived previous to Calvary.

This dynamic should not surprise us at all, for the practice of enjoying the present benefits of a covenanted object for which final payment has not yet been made is common to human experience. For example, people do this very thing when they sign a mortgage on a home, or assume an automobile loan. Do you have to wait for 30 years until the last payment has been made to move in to the house you covenanted to purchase, or are you allowed to move in the very day that the papers are signed on good-faith that the total will be paid in full? Obviously, the legally-binding, signed contract permits a person to begin to enjoy the benefits of the property even though the final payment has not yet been made.

The prophet Zechariah anticipated the cleansing efficacy of Messiah's atoning death in a powerful, poetic passage that makes the very same point: *"In that day living waters shall go out from Jerusalem, half of them toward the former sea, and half of them toward the hinder sea: in summer and in winter shall it be"* (Zech. 14:8). When Jesus Christ shed his precious blood on the cross, that blood cleansed the sins of God's elect who lived both prior to and subsequent to the redemptive transaction.

And that fountain opened to God's covenant family will never lose its cleansing power, regardless of changes in season or circumstance.

The Lord Jesus approached the cross, therefore, in a spirit of covenant obligation: *"Ought not Christ to have suffered, and entered into his glory"* (Lk. 24:26). With this mediatorial assignment in mind from earliest youth (e. g. *"Wist ye not that I must be about my Father's business?"* - Lk. 2:49), *Jehovah's Servant* "set his face like a flint" toward the cross (cf. Is. 50:7). The use of the past tense "finished" in John 17:4 therefore, even though he presently offered this prayer in Calvary's shadow, must be understood in terms of Jesus' determination to complete his covenant assignment.

Salvation from sin, therefore, is a finished work (cf. Jno. 19:30). The Lord Jesus did not merely make the elect savable or redeemable at the cross; he actually secured salvation for all that were given to him by the Father in covenant. This focus on the covenant of grace continues in verse 5.

"And now, O Father, glorify thou me with thine own self with the glory which I had with thee before the world was" (Jno. 17:5). The gift of eternal life was planned in the covenant before the foundation of the world. Further, in that covenant, the Son of God assumed the role of Mediator, agreeing to fulfill the stipulations of that covenant. Now, in the face of completing that covenant work, our Lord prays as if something is due him. He prays to be restored to his preincarnate glory with the Father.

It needs to be said that this petition does not suggest, in any sense, that Jesus ceased to be Divine at the incarnation. When he was dispatched into this world, the Son of God emptied himself of dignity, not Deity. He left his glory in heaven, not his Godhood. The change was in his position, not his Person. He was still as much God subsequent to the incarnation as he was prior to it. Yet he had divested himself of his Divine prerogatives in agreeing to assume our nature. When he assumed the humiliating posture of a servant, he released his grasp on the rights and privileges of exaltation and voluntarily subordinated himself to a role in which he was under authority.

It is precisely in this sense that we should interpret verses such as John 14:28 ("*My Father is greater than I*") and 1 Corinthians 15:28 ("*...then shall the Son be subject to the Father...*"), as well as language stating that the Father "*gave*" something to the Son (Jno. 5:26-27; Mt. 19:28), "*committed*" something to the Son (Jno. 5:22), "*appointed*" something to the Son (Heb. 1:2), or "*sent*" the Son (Jno. 10:36). The Jehovah's Witnesses (and similar cults that deny the deity of Christ) are wrong to employ these statements to imply that the Son is somehow inferior to the Father. Instead, this language must be interpreted in terms of Christ's assumed role as Mediator, not in terms of his Divine Person.

As God of very God, the Second Person was never given anything by the First Person of the Holy Trinity, but everything that is essentially true of the Father and the Spirit is also essentially true of the Son. When he volunteered to fill the role of Mediator, however, he also agreed to divest himself of his claims to heavenly honor, and to place himself in a posture of obligation to keep the conditions of the covenant. Now as he approaches the cross, however, Jesus claims that he has completed his covenant assignment, and prays to be restored to the exalted dignity and honor—the "glory," if you will—that he had enjoyed with the Father from all eternity past.

Notice that he does not say, "Father, I beg," as if he is asking for mercy, nor even, "Father, I request." He prays, *"Father, I will,"* as if glory is his unquestionable right. Was glory due to him, you ask? Absolutely, for he had *"finished the work which"* the Father had given him to do.

Again, salvation is a finished work—planned and purposed by the Father in covenant and executed and secured by the Son at the cross. And just as surely as the Father and the Son have done their part, the Holy Spirit will fulfill his covenant responsibility to vitally apply saving grace to the hearts of every respective heir of grace.

How thrilling to know that the Lord Jesus Christ did, in fact, ascend back to the Father's right hand, where he now sits enthroned as the King of saints and functions as our heavenly Priest, making intercession for the saints according to the will of God! At this very moment, Jesus intercedes in heaven, functioning in this priestly role to guarantee that the Father's will is properly probated, and that every covenant provision secured by his death is properly distributed to the beneficiaries of grace, the covenant people of God.

The Gift of God's Word: Sanctification (vs. 6-21)

The second, and largest, section of the Lord's High Priestly prayer focuses on the present needs of believers as they seek to properly represent Jesus Christ in this world. How comforting it is to know that our great High Priest is concerned with the temporal needs of his church! This part of the prayer reminds us that the daily conflicts and burdens we face as disciples of Christ in this ungodly world are matters of our risen Lord's ongoing concern.

The first part of this prayer focused on the gift of eternal life (v. 2); this second section concerns the gift of God's word (v. 8). The gift of eternal life has to do with salvation, and that work is finished (v. 4). The gift of God's word has to do with sanctification, and that work is ongoing (v. 18). This dominant section of our Lord's intercessory prayer concerns then, what we might call, the *unfinished* work of Christ.

Three pertinent questions beg an answer: Why? What? Who?. First, *why* does Jesus pray for his followers that would be left in the world when he returns to heaven? Besides the fact that the Lord Jesus felt a responsibility for these disciples who had been given to him out of the world as his personal charge (cf. v. 6), it is clear that he is burdened about the dangers that face them and the difficulties they will be called to endure (cf. vs. 14-15), as well as the important and challenging task to which they have been called in this world (cf. v. 18, 20).

Secondly, for *what* does Jesus pray on behalf of his church? Jesus highlights three specific areas in which his followers will need special help from the Father. He prays (1) that they may be *protected from the assaults of the devil* (vs. 11-16—the key word here is "keep"); (2) that they may *remain united with each other* by means of staying united to God the Father and the Lord Jesus Christ (vs. 11b, 21, 23—the key word here is "one"); and (3) That they may be *sanctified by God's word*, i.e. separated more and more from the world and consecrated more and more unto God (vs. 17, 19—the key word here is "sanctify"). In other words, Christ's priestly concern extends to the challenge of resisting the onslaught of evil, fostering unity and togetherness within the body of believers, and the development of personal Christian character in each individual heart and life.

Thirdly, *who* are the followers for whom Jesus the Priest is concerned? Obviously, this "church" is not universal, or catholic. Verse 9 indicates that this is not an indiscriminate prayer for all men in general: *"I pray for them: I pray not for the world, but for them which thou hast given me; for they are thine."* It is evident that there are certain marks or characteristics that serve to distinguish the true followers of Christ from the world at large. Do you wonder, then, how we may identify the followers of the Lord Jesus Christ? Several helpful insights

260

may be gleaned from this passage concerning the identity of Christ's true followers.

Notice the four identifying terms in verses 6-8: *received* (v. 8), *believed* (v. 8), *known* (v. 8), *kept* (v. 6). Let's discuss them one at a time.

The true followers of Jesus—and those for whom he now prays—are people, first of all, that have **received** the revelation of God's name: *"I have manifested thy name unto the men which thou gavest me out of the world...for I have given unto them the words which thou gavest me; and they have received them..."* (vs. 6a, 8a). In these verses we discover that Jesus Christ came into the world not only to save his people from their sins but also to reveal his Father's name (cf. Heb. 1:1-2; Jno. 1:18). He came, in other words, on a prophetic as well as a priestly mission—not only to redeem but to reveal redemption. The Messianic prophecy recorded in Psalm 22:22 anticipated this important role: *"I will declare thy name unto my brethren: in the midst of the congregation will I praise thee."*

Don't miss the significance of these important synonyms: *declared, manifested, revealed.* A very key part of Jesus' covenant assignment was to make his Father and his Father's counsels known. He whose name is *"the Word of God"* (Jno. 1:1ff; Rev. 19:13) is now God's *"Amen"* (Rev. 3:14) or last word. Not only is he the *"Alpha,"* the first letter of the Greek alphabet (indicating that Jesus Christ is the means by which we begin to know the true God), but he is also the *"Omega,"* the last letter of the Greek alphabet (indicating that Jesus Christ is the full and final revelation of the true God; cf. Rev. 1:8, 11; 21:6; 22:13). Jesus aimed at full disclosure of the truth of God and since the Son of God has come, revelation, like redemption, is a finished work (cf. 1 Jno. 5:20-21; Heb. 1:1-2). There is nothing remaining to be said. If we needed to know anything further, he would have told us (cf. Jno. 14:2b).[5]

"I have given them thy words and they have received them" (v. 8a). The church and the word of God are inseparably connected. It is Divine revelation—i.e. the gift of God's word —that distinguishes the church from the world. Discipleship begins when a person receives the word of God (cf. 1 Ths. 1:6).

The true followers of Jesus are identified, secondly, as people who **believe** that Jesus is God the Son: *"...and have known surely that I came out from thee, and they have believed that thou didst send me"* (v. 8b). They are people that have ceased to quibble and have embraced the Lord Jesus Christ in gospel faith, affirming Divine revelation concerning his person and work. To believe is the antithesis of an attitude of perpetual skepticism and agnosticism. In contrast to those who argue with God's word, attempt to disprove it or find some contradiction in it, the believer is someone in whose mind and

---

[5] Christian orthodoxy involves the affirmation that Scripture is complete and sufficient. No further revelation is needed by the church, nor should any be sought. Cults and fringe groups seriously err, therefore, when they insist that other literature beside God's special revelation in Scripture is necessary to fully know and comprehend God (or that the teaching of a particular leader is Divinely inspired, carrying the authority of revelation). Revelation is final in Christ and his apostles.

heart the verdict has been settled in favor of God's revelation in Scripture.

Thirdly, the true followers of Jesus may be identified as those who have **known**, or been assured of the truth of Divine revelation: *"...[they] have known that all things whatsoever thou hast given me are of thee...and have known surely that I came out from thee..."* (vs. 7, 8b). This term indicates a level of certainty and conviction concerning the identity of Jesus Christ as the Divine Son. Such a firm persuasion is indicative of authentic discipleship (cf. Jno. 6:69; 2 Tim. 1:12; Rom. 4:20).

Finally, the subjects that comprise Jesus' target audience in this middle section of the prayer are identified as those who have **kept**, or obeyed, God's word: *"...and they have kept thy word"* (v. 6b). Like the faithful remnant described in Revelation 12:17 and 14:12, these authentic disciples of Jesus are marked by both their possession of the gospel message, i.e. *"[they] have the testimony of Jesus Christ,"* and their commitment to living their lives in the light of it, i.e. *"[they] keep the commandments of God."*

We may summarize this description of Christ's followers by saying that the true followers of Jesus are people that have received a gift—the gift of God's word—and it is that truth that distinguishes them from the world in general. It is through these true followers that the Lord Jesus Christ intends to be *"glorified"* in the earth (cf. v. 10).

By what means do true believers glorify Christ in the world? Verse 18 gives us a clue: *"As thou hast sent me into the world, even so have I also sent them into the world.*" This verse indicates that just as Christ was sent into the world to glorify the Father, so the church has been sent into the world to glorify the Son. The church continues in this world subsequent to the Lord's ascension to his pre-incarnate glory with the Father for the express purpose of bringing glory to the Lord Jesus Christ.

The church, in other words, is his representative in the world (cf. Acts 1:8; 2 Cor. 5:20). Of course, the world itself does not glorify Jesus. The world ridicules the Lord Jesus Christ and blasphemes that worthy name by which we are called. No, this fallen world system does not honor Christ; it glorifies and praises people, celebrating politicians, entertainers, athletes, philosophers and entrepreneurs. If anyone presumes to magnify the matchless name of Jesus Christ, the world is offended.

The goal of Christian discipleship, then, is spelled out in these terms. The church has been left in this world to glorify Jesus Christ. This is the important task to which we have been called.

It is not, however, a simple task. We may be thankful to know, therefore, that the Lord Jesus is praying for his true followers as they seek to fulfill this high calling.

Why is it such a difficult thing to glorify Jesus Christ in the earth? It is not an easy assignment because the world is enemy territory for the church. Jesus himself affirmed this relationship of tension between the church and the world in

John 15:19: *"If ye were of the world, the world would love his own: but because ye are not of the world, but I have chosen you out of the world, therefore the world hateth you."*

Connect that verse to verses 11 (*"And now I am no more in the world, but these are in the world, and I come to thee..."*), 14 (*"...the world hath hated them, because they are not of the world, even as I am not of the world"*), and 18 (*"As thou hast sent me into the world, even so have I also sent them into the world"*), and a formula for thinking about the church emerges as follows: The church is *in* but **not of** *the world*, yet *sent* **into** *the world* to glorify Jesus Christ.

In but *not of* the world. What an important way to think about genuine believers in Jesus Christ! The believer is someone who is not of the world, for he has been called out of this world (cf. Jno. 15:19b) to live a separated life of consecration to God. The gospel calls God's born-again child to *"come out from among them and be separate"* (cf. 2 Cor. 6:17). It is a call to non-conformity: *"Be not conformed to this world but be ye transformed by the renewing of your mind..."* (Rom. 12:2).

Yet, this call to separation and consecration is not a summons to isolation. "Be separate" does not equate to monasticism—a cloistered and sequestered kind of existence —else the follower of Jesus has no opportunity to fulfill his commission to be "salt and light" in this world (cf. Mt. 5:16). Of course, salt can exercise no influence upon decaying meat while it is still in the container, neither can light dispel darkness if it is kept hidden beneath a basket. Likewise, the

Christian cannot glorify Christ in the world as long as he equates the call to holiness with a monastic life of isolation. In their zeal to be faithful to God and to keep themselves untainted by this world, so many professing Christians (not just the monks) have opted for a social ethic characterized by withdrawal, isolation, and non-involvement with popular culture. This is a grave mistake, for it negates the commission for which Jesus sends his disciples "into the world" (v. 18).

Instead, the challenge facing Christ's disciples is to live in the world while remaining true to their otherworldly identity. Maintaining this balance of living "in the world" while not belonging to it is basic and fundamental to the call to infiltrate the world with Christ's gospel as his representatives in the earth.

Because his followers are *in but not of* this world, yet have been *sent into* the world to continuing the important work of the gospel, Jesus prays to the Father for their safety: "*Holy Father, keep through thine own name those whom thou hast given me...While I was with them in the world, I kept them in thy name...I pray not that thou shouldest take them out of the world, but that thou shouldest keep them from the evil...*" (vs. 11b-12a, 15).

The repetition of this thought of "keeping" is important. The verb means "to safeguard" or "to protect." Just as a shepherd keeps his sheep by exercising vigilance concerning their needs for provision and protection, so the Lord Jesus Christ is dedicated to the believer's safety in this unfriendly world.

It should be said that Jesus is not here concerned with the eternal security of his people, else verse 12 is contradictory to the preponderance of Biblical evidence teaching that every elect is Divinely preserved in grace (cf. Jno. 6:37-39; 10:27-30). Let me explain.

John 17:12 refers to Judas Iscariot, saying, "...*those that thou gavest me I have kept, and none of them is lost, but the son of perdition; that the scripture might be fulfilled.*" Is this verse the only exception to the doctrine of Divine preservation in the Bible? No, for John 6:37-39 teaches that there is no exception to the rule: "*All that the Father giveth me shall come to me...Of all that he has given me, I should lose nothing, but raise it up again at the last day.*"

The security of every one of God's elect, redeemed and regenerate people in Christ is guaranteed. But their safety in gospel knowledge and fellowship with the saints in this world is not guaranteed. Notice that the "keeping" in view in this context is a safety "*in [the Father's] name*" (v. 12), that is, in an understanding and knowledge of God as revealed (or "*manifested*"—v. 6a) in the word. By this reference to "keeping," Jesus signals his concern that the minds of his disciples would not be deceived nor their hearts enticed and ensnared by this world. He prays "*keep them from the evil,*" which word[6] likely means "the evil one," a reference to the devil.

---

[6]When the Greek word *poneros* appears, as it does here, in the nominative case, it usually denotes a title, meaning "the Evil One." See the same word translated "that Wicked One" in 1 John 5:18.

We may infer from verse 12 that the church is never a completely perfect entity in this world. There may be those, in other words, numbered among the disciples that are not true believers but, like Judas, imposters. Such religious fakes may be used by Satan to infiltrate the church, wreaking havoc among the saints.

Jesus prays, therefore, that the heavenly Father might protect and preserve the church in the face of the many dangers that attend a life of gospel labor in the enemy territory of this world. Taking his cue from the Savior, the apostle Paul, years later, committed the safekeeping of the church of Ephesus to the Father's care: "And I commend you to God and to the word of his grace which is able to build you up..." (Acts 20:32). To be in the very capable hands of God's care and keeping is to be in a truly safe place in this world.

In a word, the basic call of discipleship to be separated from this world and consecrated to God is a call to sanctification: *"Sanctify them through thy truth: thy word is truth...and for their sakes I sanctify myself, that they also might be sanctified through the truth"* (vs. 17, 19). Our Lord's great concern for his followers is for their holiness in an unholy world.

Verse 17 concerns ethical holiness, or practical sanctification. It is talking about the way believers live and conduct themselves in the world—holy behavior, if you will. Holy behavior depends upon the instrumentality of God's

268

word; it is "sanctification by means of the truth," as verses 17 and 19 indicate.

Of course, practical sanctification should be rightly divided (or distinguished) from positional sanctification. Positional sanctification—that is, a holy posture before God—is not by means of the word of God. It is by means of the cross of Jesus Christ: *"By the which will we are sanctified by the body of Jesus Christ once for all"* (Heb. 10:10); *"But of God are ye in Christ Jesus, who of God is made unto us...sanctification...according as it is written, He that glorieth, let him glory in the Lord"* (1 Cor. 1:30).

Every one of God's elect is already perfectly holy before God by virtue of the Lord Jesus Christ. We *"are sanctified in Christ Jesus"*—the aorist tense suggesting the thought of punctiliar, definitive action (1 Cor. 1:2a). So far as our home in heaven is concerned, we are already as holy as we will ever be through Christ who has made us saints in his death.

But those given such a holy posture before God in Jesus Christ are called to be in practice what they already are in position: *"...To them that are sanctified in Christ Jesus, **called to be saints**"* (1 Cor. 1:2). How are we to understand this text that says that God's people are at the same time already saints, i.e. "are sanctified," and called to be saints? It makes perfect sense when we understand the distinction between positional (or definitive) and practical (or daily) sanctification. The gospel calls upon those who belong to Jesus Christ to be in practice what they profess to be in position—in a word, to be who they are.

Practical sanctification, or ethical holiness in daily life and conduct, does, in fact, depend upon regular exposure to the word of God. If the believer is to behave himself/herself in a holy, Christ-like way in this world, God's word will necessarily play an integral role in the arrangement.

It is simply impossible to overcome sin and temptation without daily Bible intake. It is as the believer hears the gospel preached, reads, studies and memorizes Scripture, and applies Biblical wisdom to the real world around him that he is enabled to live a holy life in this unholy world. Constant exposure to the truth of God's word is crucial to the Christian's safety from sin and the devil.

Jesus has already hinted at the invaluable resource the Bible is to those who seek to live a clean life in a dirty world: *"Now ye are clean through the word that I have spoken unto you"* (Jno. 15:4). The Psalmist likewise emphasizes this relationship between exposure to the truth of God's word and the capacity to navigate a godly path through this life: *"Wherewithal shall a young man cleanse his way? by taking heed thereto according to thy word...Thy word have I hid in my heart that I might not sin against thee"* (Ps. 119:9, 11).

Holiness of life and conduct involves becoming more spiritually mature—of "growing up into Christ" in every area of our lives (cf. Eph. 4:15). In specific terms, to be more like Jesus in terms of attitudes, thought-patterns, words, work ethic, and relational unity is the subject of that very practical passage at the end of Ephesians 4 (vs. 22-32). Holiness, in

270

other words, has to do with the way a believer thinks, talks, and interacts with others.

In Peter's epistles, Christian sanctification is framed in terms of "growth in grace" (cf. 1 Pet. 2:2; 2 Pet. 3:18). In John's, it is expressed by the imagery of "perfection in love" (cf. 1 Jno. 4:12, 17, 18). To Paul, sanctification is "spiritual transformation into Christ's likeness" (cf. Rom. 12:2; 2 Cor. 3:18). Change from the sinful habits of the past and growth toward maturity in Christian character, then, is essential to authentic discipleship.

Such change in the life of a believer is inseparably connected to God's word. As he/she reads and hears the word of God, sinful habits of mind, heart and life are exposed and repentance is urged. This negative side of the equation is called the mortification of sin. Then, on the positive side, the word holds forth the Lord Jesus Christ as the epitome of holiness. As the believer looks unto Jesus, then, the Holy Spirit works through the word to transform the individual into the image of Christ, from one degree of glory to another, so that real spiritual growth takes place. Theologians call this vivification, or consecration to God.

Second Corinthians 3:18 spells out this dynamic: *"But we all, with open face beholding as in a glass the glory of the Lord, are changed into the same image from glory to glory, even as by the Spirit of the Lord."* One preacher explained the verse as follows: When the child of God looks into the word of God and sees the Son of God, he is transformed by the Spirit of

God into the image of God, from one degree of glory to another. Just as Moses reflected God's glory after spending time with him in the holy mount, so the believer who takes time to be holy through fellowship with Jesus in the word begins to reflect that holy likeness in his own countenance and life.

This is the practical sanctification, or holiness of character and conduct, that the Lord prioritizes for believers in this world. It is the means by which they remain separated and safe from the world's evil influences, as well as by which they are equipped for service to Christ in this world. It is such a crucial part of authentic Christian discipleship that Jesus, the Priest, makes it central to his ongoing intercessory work on behalf of his church in all subsequent ages (cf. vs. 20-21). How encouraging to know that he still prays for believers today, just as he prayed for his original disciples in the first century!

In verses 22-24, the Lord Jesus transitions to the final section of his prayer, i.e. his concern for the future glory of all that were given to him by the Father in covenant. John 17:25-26, however, return to this focus on the present needs of his church: *"O righteous Father, the world hath not known thee: but I have known thee, and these have known that thou hast sent me. And I have declared unto them thy name, and will declare it: that the love wherewith thou hast loved me may be in them, and I in them."*

Don't miss the significance of this blessed clause, *"...and will declare it."* In this expression, the church in all subsequent ages may find encouragement to proclaim the gospel with indefatigable zeal, for Christ pledges to assist the effort from his heavenly throne. Here is hope for the success of the Christian evangel in a world that is antagonistic to that gospel message. And here is reason to never give up in discouragement, for Jesus Christ himself promises his own heavenly involvement in the effort to promote the message of God's sovereignty in grace.

The Gift of God's Glory—Glorification (vs. 22-24)

The final portion of Jesus' high-priestly prayer in John 17 concerns the future glory that awaits all who belong to Christ: *"And the glory which thou gavest me I have given them; that they may be one, even as we are one; I in them, and thou in me, that they may be made perfect in one; and that the world may know that thou hast sent me, and hast loved them, as thou hast loved me. Father, I will that they also, whom thou hast given me, be with me where I am; that they may behold my glory, which thou hast given me: for thou lovedst me before the foundation of the world"* (vs. 22-24). This passage indicates that final glory for all that were given to Christ by the Father is the triumphant goal of the covenant of redemption.

Of what does the glory of heaven consist? First, it consists of *perfect union with the Lord* (vs. 22-23a). In other words, the glory that awaits God's elect is perfect likeness to Jesus Christ. Does the song "Oh to be like thee, blessed Redeemer" express the deepest yearning of your soul? That longing will finally be realized.

273

Notice the emphasis on "oneness" in these verses. Jesus prays that his loved ones may realize the same perfect union with God and one another that the Father and the Son enjoy within the Godhead: *"That they all may be one; as thou, Father, art in me, and I in thee, that they also may be one in us."*

Of course, since sin entered the world, this realm has been torn apart by strife, division, war, conflict and tension. But grace aims to restore harmony—to reconcile and unite. Just as there is no disharmony within the Godhead, there will be no disunity or discord in heaven: *"And there shall in no wise enter into it any thing that defileth, neither whatsoever worketh abomination, or maketh a lie: but they which are written in the Lamb's book of life"* (Rev. 21:27).

On what basis may we expect perfect unity in heaven? Heaven will be a world of peace and concord because there will be no sin in that city. No fusses, disagreements, fights, feelings of estrangement or alienation will encroach upon that repose of that peaceful clime, for every inhabitant of that holy place will be made perfectly like Jesus Christ (cf. Phi. 3:21). The goal of sanctification will then be realized in glorification.

How thrilling is this gift of God's grace: *"I have given them thy glory"*! Jesus speaks of glorification, the grand finale of the covenant of redemption, as a present possession—as a gift already given. In what sense, wonders the believer who presently struggles to practice holiness in an unholy world, is glorification a present reality? It is so in the sense that the Father promised it in covenant and the Son procured and purchased it on the cross; consequently, the glory of heaven is just as sure as if we were already there. Compare the use of the past tense "glorified" in Romans 8:29-30 to the Savior's words here, "I have given them thy glory." Glorification, i.e. perfect likeness to and union with Christ in the presence of the Lord, is guaranteed by Divine grace.

In what else does the future glory of heaven consist? Heavenly glory is not only a matter of perfect likeness to Jesus but also of the perpetual and uninterrupted presence of Jesus: *"Father, I will that they...be with me where I am."* Heaven will be glorious because the redeemed will be *with Christ* forever, never to part again. The precious promise of John 14:3—*"I will come again and receive you unto myself, that where I am, there ye may be also"*—will finally be realized. Togetherness with Christ in paradise (cf. Lk. 23:43) is what makes that world paradise to the heir of grace. What comfort this sweet sentence affords: *"And so shall we ever be **with the Lord**"* (1 Ths. 4:17b)!

Finally, the glory of heaven consists not only of being like Jesus and being with Jesus; it also consists of **seeing Jesus** as he is: *"...that they may behold my glory, which thou hast given me"* (v. 24b). Moses' daring request for the beatific vision (*"I beseech thee, Show me thy glory"* - Ex. 33:1) will at last be granted. Then, no more will we behold him by faith, with partial and fleeting glimpses as though we saw him through a lattice, but "face to face" (cf. 1 Cor. 13:12) in all of his immediate glory and splendor. Though there is much about that world that we do not yet understand, this much is clear: *"We know that when he shall appear, we shall be like him, for we shall see him as he is"* (1 Jno. 3:2). And just one glimpse of him in glory will more than compensate for the many toils and troubles of life in this world.

Until the dawn of that happy day, the children of God and followers of Christ in this world may be comforted to know that Jesus, our great High Priest, continues to intercede at the Father's right hand, just as he prayed this prayer prior to his crucifixion and death. In his risen glory, the Savior continues to express his holy concern for their salvation, sanctification and final glorification. How wonderful to know that we have a heavenly Helper!

Chapter 20
The Trials & Crucifixion of Jesus (John 18-19)

John 18 opens with the account of Jesus' arrest in the Garden of Gethsemane (vs. 1-11). Unlike the other three Gospel accounts, however, there is no mention of his agony or his prayer that the cup might pass from him. Instead of emphasizing the sufferings of the Son of Man, John, in keeping with his focus throughout, emphasizes his sovereignty as God manifest in the flesh.

His sovereign power and authority is implicit in the exchange between Jesus and the Roman soldiers, a conversation that only John records. When the soldiers approached, the Lord Jesus asked, *"Whom seek ye?"* (v. 4). They replied *"Jesus of Nazareth."* Our Lord then said unto them, *"I am he"* and his would-be captors *"fell to the ground"* (v. 5). Again he asked *"Whom seek ye?"* and again they answered *"Jesus of Nazareth."* He replied, *"I have told you that I am he"* and he allowed them to apprehend him.

What is the significance of this exchange? Our Lord is simply demonstrating His Divine nature and their inability to exert any power over him whatsoever unless he willingly submitted himself to them. The simple affirmation *"I am"* exercised profound power over them. One little word, *ego eimi*, felled them! The overpowering exclamation indicates that he was more than Jesus of Nazareth alone. He was the Great I AM! Only God can slay men with the mere breath of his mouth. The sovereign Lord Jesus would go to the cross not as a helpless victim, but as voluntary sacrifice. His life would not be taken from him, but he would lay it down of himself (cf. 10:19).

At the moment of encounter with the Roman soldiers, Peter drew his sword to defend his Master, and inadvertantly cut off the ear of a man named Malchus (v. 10). Jesus calmly commanded him to re-sheath his sword, for he did not intend to resist arrest. Jesus fully intended to accomplish the mission given to him by the Father. We might learn from this account the important lesson that Christ's Kingdom does not advance in this world by the use of carnal weapons.

Once Jesus was in custody, the soldiers first took him to Annas, the father-in-law of the high priest Caiaphas (vs. 12-14). Annas had himself been high priest at one time, as well as five of his sons. Now his son-in-law was high priest and because he was a man of significant political power and influence, the soldiers first sought his advice.

Peter and John followed the delegation as they proceeded to the chambers of Caiaphas (v. 15). As Peter and John entered the palace, the lady that kept the door asked Peter if he was not, in fact, one of Jesus' disciples. Peter denied his affiliation with Jesus, saying *"I am not"* (v. 17). The Holy Spirit records, perhaps as an object lesson of Peter's attempt to distance himself from Jesus and to save his own skin, the fact that Peter warmed himself by the fire with the arresting delegation.

Verses 19-24 record Caiaphas' interrogation of Jesus. He questioned Jesus about his disciples and doctrine. The intention was to charge Jesus with sedition and rebellion against Caesar. In order to make the charge stick, they needed to prove that Jesus had enough disciples to make a formidable threat. The question about his doctrine was intended to coax Jesus into admitting to parts of his doctrine that might be construed as potentially subversive to the Roman government.

Our Lord responded, in effect, that nothing about his teaching ministry was secret. He did not have any secrets. He had taught publicly in the synagogue and in the temple. Any Jewish man or woman in Jerusalem could verify the things he taught. At that answer, one of the officers slapped Jesus and accused him of impudence. The Lord replied, in essence, "If I've committed perjury then explain what false thing I have said; but if I have spoken the truth, then what basis do you have to strike me?" (vs. 22-23).

In verses 25-27, Simon Peter's second and third denials are recorded. The soldiers with whom Peter stood said, "*Art not thou also one of his disciples?*" Peter again responded, "*I am not.*" Then one of Malchus' relatives asked, "*Did not I see thee in the garden with him?"* When Peter denied this allegation, immediately the cock crowed.

Caiaphas, the Jewish high priest, then sent Jesus, probably around 6 a.m., to Pilate, the Roman governor (vs. 28-37). At Pilate's judgment hall, Pilate asked about the charge (v. 29). The soldier's answer was evasive, and a classic example of both the "bandwagon" and "begging the question" logical fallacies: *"If he were not a malefactor, we would not have delivered him up unto thee"* (v. 30). When Pilate expressed his reluctance to get involved in Jewish legal affairs, *"Take ye him and judge him according to your law"* (v. 31), they responded by framing their case against Jesus in capital terms, reminding the Roman governor that as a vassal nation, they were not permitted to prosecute capital cases: *"It is not lawful for us to put any man to death"* (v. 31b).

The brief hearing that followed consisted of Pilate asking Jesus if he was, in fact, the King of the Jews (v. 33). Evidently, that was the official charge on which he had been arraigned, and the Jewish religious leaders intended by that charge to suggest that Jesus was posturing himself as a rival to Caesar. Jesus responded that his kingdom was not of this world, essentially denying the charge (v. 36). As evidence for his claim, he cites an example of how his kingdom differed from earthly kingdoms. The kingdoms of men depend on arms and armies to defend them against enemies. The subjects of his kingdom, however, do not fight with carnal weapons.

Indeed, the kingdom of Jesus Christ is a heavenly and spiritual, not a worldly and political, kingdom (cf. Rom. 14:17; Jno. 3:3ff). Pilate then repeated the question, *"Art thou a king then?"* Jesus replied, *"Thou sayest I am a King."* This obtuse expression is equivalent to an affirmation, and to this Paul has reference when he reminds Timothy that Jesus unashamedly *"witnessed a good confession"* before Pontius Pilate (1 Tim. 6:13).

Instead of posing a political threat to Caesar, Jesus then adds this explanation of the purpose of his public ministry: *"To this end was I born, and for this cause came I into the world, that I should bear witness unto the truth. Every one that is of the truth heareth my voice"* (v. 37). Pilate's response reveals his own personal skepticism and cynical preference for philosophical relativism: *"What is truth?"*

At this passing retort, Pilate returned to the Jewish leaders claiming that he *"found no fault in him at all"* (v. 38). The initial hearing had yielded no evidence consistent with the capital charge made by the Jewish rulers. But the Jews were undeterred. Because they had a tradition of requesting the release of one prisoner from the Romans at Passover, Pilate suggested that the release of Jesus might be a convenient way for them to save face, that is to save face for condemning a man to death without sufficient evidence, as well as to satisfy the custom.

So intense was their malice, however, they cried, *"Not this man, but Barabbas"* (v. 40). Barabbas, the robber, was subsequently set free, and Jesus was taken to be scourged.

The Crucifixion (Jno. 19)

John 19 records the historical facts of this pivotal moment in human history, i.e. the crucifixion of the Lord Jesus Christ. The epistles, subsequently, will explain the theological significance of this historical event.

Jesus and the Politician (vs. 1-16)

At the violent and vitriolic insistence of the Jewish mob, therefore, Pilate reluctantly began the ugly proceedings of crucifixion, a Roman method of punishing capital offenders, by scourging Jesus (v. 1). Scourging involved the merciless whipping of a subject scheduled to be crucified. It was intended to add to the horrors of the punishment and to inflict even greater suffering. The procedure left Jesus' back, buttocks and thighs in ribbons of bloody flesh, in fulfillment of the Messianic prophecy, *"The plowers plowed upon my back: they made long their furrows"* (Ps. 129:3).

After the Roman soldiers mocked him as "King" by weaving together a crown of thorns and draping him with a purple robe, Pilate, the Roman Governor of Judea, made one final appeal to the angry mob, affirming once more that he had found no fault in him. Pilate intended to move them to pity and compassion with his statement, *"Behold the man"* (v. 5).

It is noteworthy that the Lord Jesus never opened his mouth in his own defense. He bore every humiliation and indignity with meekness and patience. Pilate wanted them to see that this calm and gentle man they had accused was not guilty. But they were unmoved. None eye pitied the innocent Lamb of God. *"Crucify him, crucify him!"* they demanded (v. 6).

Pilate would have none of it. He told the chief priests that if they wanted Jesus crucified, then they would have to do it, for he had already declared him innocent (v. 6b). The chief priests and Pharisees then brought a new charge against Jesus – the charge of blasphemy: *"We have a law, and by our law he ought to die, because he made himself the Son of God"* (v. 7). This charge of blasphemy was not the original charge on which they had arraigned him before Pilate. They had accused him originally of sedition, and Pilate had declared him innocent of such a charge. Since they could not secure a conviction on the charge of sedition, the Jewish rulers now accused him of the same charge on which they had arraigned and condemned him before the Sanhedrin—the charge of blasphemy.

This new charge heightened Pilate's awareness of the extreme malice and animosity that the Jewish leaders harbored against Jesus, and the extent to which they were willing to go to destroy the polarizing teacher (v. 8). And Pilate realized for the first time the serious implications of this situation. The Jews were requesting State intervention for a religious crime. Their own religious law demanded capital punishment for blasphemy, but they could not carry out the sentence themselves since they were under Roman jurisdiction.

Pilate faced both a moral and a political dilemma *par excellence*. If he complied, he effectively involved Rome in the immoral condemnation of an innocent man. If he resisted, he jeopardized his own political career, for the mob was on the verge of a very public riot and rebellion.

Pilate retired once more to the Praetorium to examine Jesus. *"Whence art thou?"* he asked Jesus. Where did you come from? *"But Jesus gave him no answer"* (v. 9). He had already answered Pilate's question (cf. 18:33-37). He had already established his innocence and satisfied Pilate of that fact. His refusal to answer now has the effect of a rebuke to Pilate for his lack of resolve to do what his conscience convinced him was morally right. It also suggests an important spiritual principle, namely that our Lord is unwilling to give further light to someone who fails to act on the light they've already been given.

The Lord Jesus knew that after establishing his innocence and being so mercilessly beaten and mocked, he had no basis on which to expect justice at Pilate's hands. Hence, the Lamb of God opened not his mouth (cf. Is. 53:7).

Proud Pilate scolded Jesus: *"Speakest thou not to me? Knowest thou not that I have power to crucify thee, and have power to release thee?"* (v. 10). Jesus replied that Pilate's authority (like the power of every earthly leader) was a delegated authority from an even Higher Power: *"Thou couldest have no power at all against me, except it were given thee from above: therefore he that delivered me unto thee hath the greater sin"* (v. 11).

Albert Barnes comments, "Alas! How many men in office forget that God gives them their rank, and vainly think that it is owing to their own talents or merits that they have risen to that elevation. Men of office and talent, as well as others, should remember that God gives them what they have and that they have no influence except as it is conceded to them from on high."[1]

Our Lord's words do not exonerate Pilate of culpability, but admit that those who put him in such a precarious position, essentially forcing the State to participate in an immoral act, have the greater guilt. Of course, Pilate could have exonerated himself and the Roman Empire he represented from any guilt by simply releasing Jesus. Indeed, it would have cost him his political career. The riots and insurrection that would have resulted from his refusal to participate in this mockery of justice would likely result in Caesar relieving him of his post and any political aspirations he might have had for the throne himself would be history. But wouldn't the sacrifice of personal ambition be a small price to pay for a clear conscience?

Would Pilate do the right thing and sacrifice his own career for the sake of truth and justice and morality, or would he play the politician and compromise to save his own skin? All hope that he would play the man and establish precedent for

---

[1] *Barnes Notes on the New Testament*, p. 353.

honor in political office was lost when he buckled to the pressure and presented Jesus once more to the multitude saying, *"Behold your King"* (v. 14).

The actual crucifixion and death of Jesus is the theme of verses 17-37. John does not record the detail of the event with as much specificity as the other Gospel writers. He focuses primarily, however, on two intriguing observations that the other Gospels omit: (1) Jesus' concern for his earthly mother; (2) Jesus' early death after only six hours on the cross.

Providing for His Mother (vs. 25-27)

It is significant that the Lord Jesus Christ took care to provide for the ongoing provision of his earthly mother as he hung upon the cross. One would think that he might be too preoccupied with his own sufferings, or too focused on the redemptive task in which he was engaged to even notice such a comparatively mundane detail as his mother's ongoing financial and domestic needs.

Nonetheless, he saw her and tenderly exhorted, *"Woman, behold thy son!"*, directing her gaze upon John. Then turning to John, he said, *"Behold thy mother."* John records that in response to this verbal instruction from the lips of the Lord upon the cross, he took her in as a member of his own family from that very hour onward (v. 27). Extra-biblical tradition says that Mary continued to live with John in Judea until the time of her death, approximately fifteen years after the death of Jesus.

What may we learn from this surprising side-note to the crucifixion? We learn that service to God does not exempt a person from caring for his own family and loved ones.

Periodically, I encounter people who are so "spiritual" that they completely neglect their own families. How many preachers have followed what they believed to be the call of God upon their lives, only to abandon their responsibilities at home in the process. Paul instructs Timothy that a Christian who provides not for his own is worse than an infidel. I seriously doubt that, short of the grace of glorification, I will be so spiritually mature that I will be exempted from ministering to the physical needs of those who are closest to me. May God protect us all from an exaggerated sense of our own importance.

Already Dead (vs 28-37)

John records two more of Jesus' seven sayings on the cross.[2] Both were recorded at the conclusion of the three hours of darkness. The first was the cry, "*I thirst*" (cf. Ps. 69:21).

It is likely that Jesus was expressing physical thirst, for "thirst was one of the most distressing circumstances attending the crucifixion".[3] It also seems plausible that his cry has a spiritual significance. On the cross, the Lord Jesus was

---

[2] The 7 statements on the cross are: "*Father forgive them*; *Today thou shalt be with me in paradise*; *Woman, behold thy son*; *My God, my God, why hast thou forsaken me?*; *I thirst*; *It is finished*;" and "*Father into thy hands I commend my spirit.*"
[3] *Barnes' Notes on the New Testament*, p. 354.

drinking the dregs of the cup of Divine wrath for sinners. He was experiencing, as it were, the flames of punishment on behalf of all who were given to him by the Father. In the heat of that bitter suffering, he longed for refreshment from the torment.

Then he cried, *"It is finished: and he bowed his head, and gave up the ghost"* (v. 30). Verses 31-37 record the surprise of the soldiers when they came to break the legs of the malefactors in order to hasten their death. Jesus was *"dead already, [so] they broke not his legs"* (v. 33).

Crucifixion was an extremely slow and agonizing method of death. The fact that Jesus was already dead indicates that he laid down his life (cf. 10:18). No man had taken it from him.

One of the soldiers pierced his side with a sword. The fact that the plasma had separated from the blood indicates that he had been dead already for at least one-half hour. In each of these events, Old Testament prophecies were fulfilled, including *"A bone of him shall not be broken"* and *"They shall look on him whom they pierced"* (vs. 36-37).

Buried in a Borrowed Tomb (vs. 38-42)

The crucifixion narrative concludes with the account of one of the Pharisees who was a secret disciple of Jesus, Joseph of Arimathea, begging his body and burying it in his own new tomb.

Another secret disciple, Nicodemus (cf. Jno 3), brought the items necessary to prepare the body for burial. Together they took his body and prepared it for burial (v. 40).

Why did Jesus have a *borrowed* tomb? Because he wouldn't need it for long. The words of verse 41, "...*wherein never man was yet laid*," are theologically significant. They suggest the uniqueness of his death. The Lord Jesus died a death that no one else could have died, a substitutionary sacrifice for his elect people, and accomplished by that death something that only he could have accomplished.

Chapter 21
The Resurrection of Jesus (John 20-21)

L ike Matthew 28, Mark 16, and Luke 24, the 20th chapter of
John's Gospel records the historical event of the bodily
resurrection of Jesus. The narrative is fundamentally credible,
for it is told from the vantage point of the disciples' surprise,
as they attempt to make sense of what it all means.

John 20:1-10 reads as a report from the vantage point of the
empty tomb, not as a detailed explanation of what happened.
We are told what they saw and left to wonder at the mystery
of how the event actually occurred. We are told simply that
Mary Magdalene, Peter, and John found the stone rolled away
and the tomb vacated with nothing but the burial clothes left
behind. Faced with this fact, these three are left to grapple
with the question of what it all means, *"for as yet they knew not
the Scripture, that he must rise again from the dead"* (v. 9).

Why does the narrative omit the details and explanation of
exactly how the resurrection of Jesus happened? Why does
John simply tell the story from the human vantage point of
what they found at their arrival upon the scene? Because the
answer to these questions is a mystery.

The resurrection of Jesus Christ is a miracle, a supernatural display of the power of God and no attempt to explain the event in scientific terms so that all mystery is removed is possible. In fact, had John attempted to tell the story from the Divine side, it would have read like something dubious and apocryphal.

The remainder of John 20 is concerned with the significance and implications of Jesus' resurrection. What does the resurrection mean? The question is answered in the three post-resurrection appearances of the Lord Jesus Christ that John cites, and summarized in verse 31: *"But these are written that ye might believe that Jesus is the Christ, the Son of God; and that believing ye might have life through his name."*

This verse means that the resurrection is the ultimate proof of the Deity of Jesus. The purpose of John throughout his Gospel has been to establish evidences for the claim that Jesus is the Son of God. The greatest of these evidences is the empty tomb (cf. Rom. 1:4).

The individual who disbelieves in Jesus will be hard pressed to explain away the empty tomb. If there was any doubt concerning Jesus' true identity prior to John 20, all doubt is eradicated by this consummate evidence, validated by eyewitnesses.

The three post-resurrection appearances of the risen Savior also demonstrates the contemporary relevance of the resurrection. Here is a message for the sad, the fearful, and the skeptical—three characteristics of the modern mood and mentality.

Appearance to Mary Magdalene (vs. 11-18)

The emotionally charged scene recorded in verses 11-18 speaks with relevance to every broken heart. Mary Magdalene gives every hint of a depressed state of mind. She weeps profusely. She seems lost, without direction of what to do next. Even her obtuse reference to some unknown "they" (v. 13) suggests her forlorn condition. When someone that she assumes is the gardener asks why she is crying, she skips the details and simply says, "*Sir if thou has born him hence, tell me where thou hast laid him*" (v. 15), simply assuming that he must know to whom she has reference.

Jesus' revelation of himself as the One who was dead, but behold, is alive forevermore had the effect of assuaging her deep grief. To all in sorrow and hopeless despair, the resurrection of Jesus is profoundly significant. It means that the risen Christ may at any moment appear to reveal his personal presence to his struggling child.

Appearance to the Disciples (vs. 19-23)

Verses 19-23 concern the second post-resurrection appearance of Jesus. It was the very same day, at evening, while the disciples were gathered in that same upper room, huddled in fear that the people who crucified Jesus would soon come for them.

While the doors were shut, Jesus suddenly appeared, speaking words of peace (v. 19). He then commissioned them as his envoys to the world (v. 21), breathing upon them in a sort of acted prophecy, anticipating what would happen to them on Pentecost morning (v. 22).

This appearance to the fearful disciples suggests that the risen Christ may at any moment appear for the sake of speaking peace to his people and enabling them for ministry.

Appearance to Thomas (vs. 24-29)

The final post-resurrection appearance recorded in John 20 is Jesus' return visit to his disciples eight days later (vs. 24-29). This time, Thomas is present. He had been skeptical of the report from his colleagues, so Jesus makes a special appearance for his sake, to help his unbelief.

I find it extremely significant that the risen Christ does not speak words of recrimination to Thomas. Instead he stoops to help the doubter and condescends to his disciple's own weakness. Upon seeing his Savior, Thomas makes what is perhaps the simplest, yet most profound, confession of faith in all the Bible: *"My Lord and my God."* May every Christian take his cue from Thomas to confess the sovereign lordship of the Savior of sinners.

The Book's Purpose Statement (vs 30-31)

Verses 30-31 record the dominant purpose statement of the book: *"...These are written, that ye might believe that Jesus is the*

Christ, the Son of God; and that believing ye might have life through his name." Each of the miracles and episodes recorded in John's Gospel has aimed at this target, i.e. to prove the Deity of the Lord Jesus Christ. The empty tomb and testimony of eyewitnesses to his resurrection is, again, the ultimate proof or evidence that Jesus is Divine.

Some Bible students cite verse 31 to argue that man's act of believing is instrumental in the matter of receiving eternal life. It is important to remember the preponderance of Biblical evidence, however, for the fact that belief in Jesus Christ is an effect, not a cause—an evidence, not the means—of eternal life. Birth necessarily precedes belief (and regeneration necessarily precedes faith) as life necessarily precedes action.

If verse 31 does not teach that believing in Jesus is the condition of eternal salvation, then how are we to interpret this language? We interpret it by remembering the things we've learned throughout this survey of John's Gospel. We have learned that belief in Jesus as the unique Son of God is described in Johannine literature both as evidence of eternal life (1:11-13; 3:15-18,36; 5:24; 11:25-26; 1 Jno. 5:1,10) and as the means by which one experiences the joys and abundance of that life even now (6:35,40; 7:38; 12:46; 14:12; 20:31).

Jesus' Third Post-Resurrection Appearance (Jno. 21)

Just as the second appearance of the risen Christ to his disciples was primarily for the sake of one person, i.e. Thomas, so the third appearance seems principally designed for the sake of one person. This time that individual is Peter. The restoration of Peter after his denial of the Lord, and his recommission for ministry is the dominant theme of John 21.

Peter's Restoration (vs. 1-14)

I find it curious that Peter, even after the risen Christ had revealed himself to the disciples, decided to return to his former occupation: *"I go a fishing"* (21:3a). It is very likely that he feels that his sin in denying Christ has disqualified him for ministry.

Discouragement and disobedience is contagious: *"...they say unto him, We also go with thee"* (21:3b). How important it is for believers to consider the effect their decisions will have on others! Every time a Christian professor deviates from the path of discipleship in favor of secular and worldly interests, he risks the sin of causing someone else, especially those who are weak in the faith, to stumble. Neighbor love, the second great commandment (cf. Mt. 22:39), demands that we assume some level of responsibility for our brothers and sisters in Christ, and attempt to motivate them toward greater commitment to Christ (cf. Heb. 10:24).

After a night of no success, the disciples spotted a figure on the shore. This unknown man asked them if they had caught any fish. When they replied with a frustrated "No," he urged them to cast the net on the right side of the boat and their fortunes would change (vs. 4-6a).

Experienced fishermen, like Simon Peter, were probably none too fond of unsolicited advice from spectators. But Peter had once before taken counsel from Jesus, the great fish-Finder, with much success (cf. Lk. 5:4-6). It is likely that on this occasion he suddenly remembered that episode when the net filled up with a multitude of fish. John confirmed Peter's suspicions, exclaiming *"It is the Lord"* and Peter responded by casting himself into the sea to swim the approximately one-hundred yards to shore (vs. 6b-7). The others disciples followed him in the boat with their mammoth catch (v. 8).

When they arrived on shore, they found breakfast already prepared (v. 9). The Lord Jesus, who is the Divine Son of God, had already prepared fish and bread for his weary disciples. He invited them with gracious words, *"Come and dine"* (v. 12).

The lesson is clear. The resurrected Christ is still in the business of providing for his servants. Even when all of their professional experience fails them, as it did Peter on this occasion, the Lord's resources to care for his disciples are not restricted. The Master of oceans and earth and skies knows how to take care of and provide for his own.

As Jesus then assumes the role, once again, of "the gracious Host," distributing bread and fish to his disciples, he turns his attention to Simon Peter.

Peter's Recommission (vs. 15-24)

Jesus asked Peter three times, *"Simon, son of Jonas, lovest thou me?"* On each occasion Peter replied *"Yea, Lord; thou knowest that I love thee."* And on each occasion, our Lord replied with the charge, *"Feed my lambs"* (or *"Feed my sheep"*).

It has been suggested that Jesus asked him three times to confirm his love for the Savior because Peter had denied Jesus three times on the night of his arrest. That is very likely.

Interestingly, Jesus employs a different term when posing the question the third time. Initially he asked, "Peter, do you *agapao* (the word for the sacrificial kind of love that God displayed to his people) me?" Peter replied, "Lord, I *phileo* (the word for filial or brotherly love) you." The third time, however, Jesus asked "Peter, do you *phileo* me?" The Lord who remembers our frame and knows that we are dust condescends to the capacities of his children and accepts their sincere intentions (cf. 2 Cor. 8:12).

"Forgive the song that falls so low beneath the gratitude I owe;
It means thy praise, however poor; An angels song can do no more."

The thrice-repeated commission to *"Feed my sheep"* is the charge for future ministry that Jesus gives to his penitent disciple. How wonderful that Jesus does not dismiss Peter from useful service because of his momentary lapse! In fact, far from demoting him, Jesus continues to employ him in public ministry. It was Peter, the pardoned denier, who would be the leading gospel spokesman on the Day of Pentecost (cf. Acts 2).

This passage also teaches that love for Christ is the ultimate motivation in Christian ministry. The best proof of your love for the Lord Jesus is a lifetime of sacrificial service to his people.

We may also glean from this passage the proper attitude that a minister is to have toward his people and other ministers. He is to see the Lord's people as "sheep" who need the tender care of a shepherd. And he is to see other ministers as servants who are ultimately accountable to Christ, not their fellows, for the way they carry out their particular calling and commission (cf. vs. 18-24).

There were many other things that Jesus did that John does not record (v. 25). Perhaps heaven will be filled with a more comprehensive survey. Until then, these are recorded by Divine Inspiration for the sake of people like us so that we may truly believe and experience the abundant life.

So, do you believe that Jesus Christ is the Son of the living God? With such abundant evidence available in the *Gospel of John*, isn't it time that you cease to quibble, vacillate and leave the question in perpetual abeyance, saying with Thomas in an unashamed confession of gospel faith, *"My Lord and my God"*? To such as believe and receive the Lord Jesus Christ in faith, God gives assurance of prior regeneration and the right to claim identity among the true followers of Christ in this world.

www.ingramcontent.com/pod-product-compliance
Lightning Source LLC
Chambersburg PA
CBHW031239090426
42742CB00007B/245